Y0-CAS-897

POLICE VEHICULAR PURSUITS

ABOUT THE AUTHOR

Doctor Hicks is currently an associate professor of criminal justice at Loyola University in New Orleans. A graduate of Michigan State University's School of Criminal Justice, Dr. Hicks also holds masters degree in psychology and criminal justice from Illinois State University. She has published on such topics as police vehicular pursuits, skinhead neo-Nazi gangs, and police operations and administration. Professor Hicks teaches research methods, statistics, and program planning and evaluation at Loyola University New Orleans. Her areas of interest within the field of criminal justice include quantitative methods, police vehicular pursuits, law enforcement administration, and white supremacy.

POLICE VEHICULAR PURSUITS

Constitutionality, Liability and Negligence

By

WENDY L. HICKS, Ph.D.

Department of Criminal Justice
Loyola University
New Orleans, Louisiana

CHARLES C THOMAS • PUBLISHER, LTD.
Springfield • Illinois • U.S.A.

Published and Distributed Throughout the World by

CHARLES C THOMAS • PUBLISHER, LTD.
2600 South First Street
Springfield, Illinois 62794-9265

©2007 by CHARLES C THOMAS • PUBLISHER, LTD.

ISBN 978-0-398-07760-0(hard)
ISBN 978-0-398-07761-7 (pbk.)

Library of Congress Catalog Card Number: 2007012286

Printed in the United States of America
MM-R-3

Library of Congress Cataloging in Publication Data

Hicks, Wendy L.
    Police vehicular pursuits : constitutionality, liability, and negligence / by
Wendy L. Hicks.
        p. cm.
    Includes bibliographic references and index.
    ISBN 978-0-398-07760-0 (hard)– ISBN 978-0-398-07761-7 (pbk.)
    1. Tort liability of police–United States. 2. Police pursuit driving–Law and
legislation–United States. I. Title.

KF1307.H53 2007
344.7305'232–dc22   2007012286

PREFACE

This book was written in an effort to fill a gap in the existing body of knowledge in the field of policing and law enforcement. As our nation's roadways continue to grow ever more congested, the myriad of legal and administrative issues inherent in police vehicular pursuits have never been more salient. To date there is no offering that attempts to assemble the many findings of previous research into the area of vehicular pursuit and the resulting liability and negligence that often accompany such operations. Research conducted on police vehicular pursuits has important ramifications for other areas of law enforcement, especially that involving the use of force. Legal rulings resulting from instances of pursuit can impact other areas of law enforcement and serve to heighten the legal risks for most contemporary law enforcement organizations. This is a timely and important topic with few textbook offerings.

W.L.H.

CONTENTS

POLICE VEHICULAR PURSUITS

Chapter 1

PUBLIC AND POLICE POLICY

In an effort to understand and appreciate the theoretical concepts governing police policy, it is perhaps best to begin with a brief discussion of public policy. The American public envisions many things when the topic of public policy is broached: military activities, social security, welfare, agricultural subsidies, or medical expenditures. Congressional representatives, presidents, governors, administrators, and even lobby groups create policy. Stated more fundamentally, public policy "is the sum of the activities of governments, whether acting directly or through agents, as it has an influence on the lives of citizens" (Peters, 1982, p. 4). Public policy has also been defined as "a course of action intended to accomplish some end" (Heclo, 1972, p. 85). In addition, Eulau and Prewitt maintained that policy is "a standing decision characterized by behavioral consistency and repetitiveness" both by those who create it and those who abide by it (Eulau & Prewitt, 1971, p. 465).

Public policy is cumulative and incremental. It is concerned more with the long-term rather than a short-term guide for behavior. Although much of the popular media attention is directed toward critiquing the federal government and its many and varied policies, it must be understood that in the United States, with a federal system of government, there are a large number of subsidiary governments also creating policy and making decisions. In a perfect political environment every subsidiary government would cooperate with every other to create consistent programs and policies. However, the actions of the many governments existing within the United States are often in conflict with one another.

It is also important to remember that not all government policies are implemented by government employees, whether at the federal or state level. Many government policies are implemented in the private sector by organizations or by individuals. This must be understood if an excessively narrow definition of public policy is to be avoided. Public policy does not concern only those programs that are directly administered in the public sector.

As this brief introduction to the intricacies of public policy comes to a close it is vital to turn now to the domain of police policy. Police policy is but one facet of public policy. Where public policy is concerned with the provision of many services and programs to society, police policy is concerned primarily with the provisions of law enforcement and order maintenance services. Public policy makes police services possible, while police policy ensures that this provision of services is in accord with the laws and mores of a democratic society.

In a democratic form of government, the state is considered subservient to the citizens. The purpose of government is to provide the citizenry with services and programs if society is to progress economically and technologically. Although the legislative functions of government remain with the citizens, the executive and judicial functions are, by necessity, rendered by special instruments of the government which remain subordinate to the people (Rousseau, 1948).

Thus, policing is far more than simply enforcing the laws of the land. Designed after the English system, American policing is performed by a variety of federal, state, and local agencies falling under civilian control. For the most part, state laws govern the activities of the police within jurisdiction of any particular state. As noted by George Cole and Christopher Smith (2001), state laws entrusted with the creation of sheriff's offices and local police forces emanate from state constitutions and statutes. Police administration as a function of government exists primarily in the abstract as individual agencies generally operate as autonomous units (Cole & Smith, 2001). Therefore, while the United States has a system for policing its society, it does not have a national police system such as those existing in many European and Asian countries. The system of policing in America is "the sum total of the efforts put forth by each of the multitude of agencies" (Kennedy, 1972, p. 7).

Fundamentally, police administration has been defined as "the organization, personnel, practices, and procedures essential to effective performance of the law enforcement and other traditional police functions by those agencies to which responsibility has been entrusted" (Marx, 1963, p. 7). This definition embraces all of the activities of the federal, state, and local governments related to execution of the police function.

Guidelines and policies for proper police administration are developed by the U.S. Constitution, city charters, state statutes, and local ordinances (Cole & Smith, 2001). While officers and administrators find themselves adhering to a host of Supreme Court decisions and Constitutional provisions, local legislative bodies also develop guidelines and requisites administrators are obliged to follow. In addition, internal policies provide guidelines for officers and administrators alike as to the proper and effective performance of daily duties. To complicate an administrator's role, modifications of existing policies and guidelines must be continuous as public pressure, political concerns, and court decisions generate new, more contemporary policies, highlighting freedom and liberty of the citizenry.

While the realm of police administration has been defined, the term "policy" is also want of an operational definition. According to Nicolaidis and Donner (1960), "Policy is a rule for action, manifesting or clarifying specific organizational goals, objectives, values, or ideals and often prescribing the obligatory or most desirable ways and means for their accomplishment. Such a rule for action established for the purpose of framing, guiding, or directing organizational activities including decision-making intends to provide relative stability, consistency, uniformity, and continuity in the operations of the organization" (p. 74).

As Pfiffner has noted, the preceding definition implies that policy is both "flexible and stable, and dynamic and static" (1960, p. 127). Policy is developed at all levels of the police organization. The chief alone does not have sole responsibility for forming and approving organizational policy. It is true that broad policies become formalized when approved by the chief, but there are many more interested parties in the primary development of policy than simply the chief. Smaller policies relating to specific functions of police operations may or may not require approval of the chief, depending on the agency. They may be formalized through approval of an appropriate command officer.

PURSUIT POLICY DEFINITIONS

Due to the fact that there exist many different definitions of police pursuits, it is, perhaps, wise to provide a few working definitions of a pursuit utilized by researchers in the past. Alpert (1987) has defined a police vehicular pursuit as:

> an active attempt by a law enforcement officer operating a vehicle with emergency equipment to apprehend a suspected law violator in a motor vehicle, when the driver of the vehicle attempts to avoid apprehension. (p. 299)

In a similar tone, Alpert and Fridell (1992) have defined a vehicular pursuit as:

> the driver of a vehicle is aware that an officer driving a police vehicle with emergency lights and siren is attempting to apprehend him or her and the driver of this vehicle attempts to avoid apprehension by increasing speed or taking other evasive actions or refuses to stop. (p. 124)

Some consensual elements can be observed in the two definitions. However, each could be coupled to provide a more thorough definition. Therefore, a more inclusive definition is preferable. For the purpose of this text the definition provided by the National Highway Traffic Safety Administration (NHTSA) and the International Association of Chiefs of Police (IACP) will be used to operationalize the term "pursuit." The NHTSA and IACP define pursuit as:

> An event that is initiated when a law enforcement officer, operating an authorized emergency vehicle, gives notice to stop (either through the use of visual or audible emergency signals or a combination of emergency devices) to a motorist who the officer is attempting to apprehend, and the motorist fails to comply with the signal by either maintaining his or her speed, increasing speed, or taking other evasive action to elude the officer's continued attempts to stop the motorist. (1995, p. 1)

CONSTITUTIONAL AND LEGAL ASPECTS

The field of police vehicular pursuits is replete with complex, often conflicting, legal issues. The consequences of negligence can have far-reaching implications for law enforcement agencies as well as individual officers. Litigation can be financially devastating for both department and officer. The need for comprehensive pursuit policy is never so evident as in an examination of many recent legal decisions. Administrators and policymakers need to continually update policy so as to effect any revisions necessary to take into consideration recent court rulings. While this is not an appropriate venue for an in-depth legal analysis of pursuit ramifications, the synopses in following chapters will provide the discriminating reader with a guide to understanding the many legal intricacies involved in police pursuits.

Many scholars maintain that the primary issue facing contemporary law enforcement administrators and individual patrol officers rests on elements pertaining directly to Fourth Amendment seizure standards. Some legal experts have posited that a suspect becomes "seized" at the instant a pursuit is initiated (Urbonya, 1987). It becomes a question of a "psychological" seizure of the suspect. Others maintain a more conservative position, with the seizure of a suspect not occurring until the termination of a pursuit (Payne, 1997). Whatever the position of experts and public authorities, it is obvious that law enforcement administrators have a difficult task in developing effective and efficient written pursuit policy so as to better protect the suspect, patrol officer, and the general public from harm. As iterated previously, a well developed pursuit policy also serves to protect the department from unsubstantiated claims of negligence and liability.

FUTURE CHAPTERS

This book is intended for the student or administrator of criminal justice and law enforcement to grasp the many intricate concepts currently facing administrators, patrol officers, and scholars in the field. The book is not intended to read as a complete legal analysis of every case processed regarding police vehicular pursuits. The legal cases contained within the text of this book are those suits in which a broader, sweeping change in policy was effected. These cases involved loss of life, deprivation of civil rights, or substantial property damage. In the vernacular, these are the cases that "made the news."

In subsequent chapters are to be found in-depth examination of previous scholarly research, analyses of liability and negligence, state tort law, federal liability law, use of force, and the most recent developments of the possibility of a national pursuit policy. Chapter 2 will outline previous scholarly research, legal aspects underlying police pursuits, and many policy considerations. It is here that the reader will discover what past researchers have identified as the most relevant factors involved in the initiation, duration, and termination of a pursuit. In addition, many important legal conceptualizations are also included as are relevant policy considerations for law enforcement administrators and patrol officers.

Chapter 3 is devoted to the exploration of liability and negligence. This chapter includes such topics as proximate cause, municipal liability, breach of reasonableness, policy elements, training, barriers to liability, breach of duty, and deliberate indifference. This chapter is an excellent tool for readers to ascertain the myriad of intricate details involved in claims of liability or negligence. It is also a way for readers to grasp the difficulty of writing good policy and training patrol officers in effective pursuit tactics.

The contents of Chapter 4 concern the issues related to state tort law. Here the discussion centers on strict liability, intentional tort, public duty, contributory negligence, assumption of risk, and sudden peril. Legal cases will be included in which state law, rather than federal law, was the cause for litigation.

Chapter 5 contains elements of federal liability law directly pertaining to police vehicular pursuits. Readers can begin to understand and appreciate the complexity and subsequent growth of the federal statutes as related to police pursuits. The Civil Rights Act of 1871, color of law, Constitutional rights violations, 42 USC § 1983, absolute immunity, qualified immunity, and good faith are each explored as directly related to the realm of police pursuits.

Police pursuits, by their very nature, involve the use of the patrol car. Quite often it is incumbent upon the pursuing officer to use the patrol car as an instrument of deadly force. Therefore, Chapter 6 explores the use of force that is involved in police pursuits. Many scholars consider the patrol car a tool as deadly, or more deadly, than the firearm, so often involved in police litigation. Chapter 6 is a synopsis of deadly force litigation and law enforcement issues that will aid the discriminating reader in understanding the complexity of police pursuits and the difficulty faced by patrol officers as they partake in pursuits during the course of their regular daily operations.

Chapter 7, the final chapter, is devoted to the national pursuit policy and concluding remarks. This chapter contains information pertaining to the possibility, feasibility, and desirability of a national pursuit policy. This idea, while certainly not new, has come into the forefront recently as an increasing number of police pursuits continue to end in tragedy. As the body count rises, law enforcement administrators have begun to debate the merits of a national, more standardized, pursuit policy in a more serious fashion. This chapter will explore the issues surrounding this possibility.

CONCLUDING REMARKS

As iterated in the opening paragraphs of this chapter, there have been numerous efforts to arrive at effective and efficient written policy in an effort to decrease the danger so often associated with police vehicular pursuits. Research has indicated that many officers repeatedly voice approval for pursuits, stating that they are an important and integral part of law enforcement's efforts to apprehend and bring to justice suspected violators of the law. The one constant in all pursuit research continues to be the necessity for comprehensive and effective policy. Administrators must constantly be aware of recent court rulings on pursuit litigation. Updated, effective policy can protect the department, officer, and public from risks involved with negligence, liability, and needless danger.

Despite the variation in rates of accidents, injuries, and fatalities, police pursuits, nonetheless, have been identified and supported by researchers and officers alike, as a necessary and integral component of police work. Routine vehicular pursuits serve to apprehend numerous wanted felons and dangerous suspects. In a study by Payne (1993), it was observed that 24.3 percent of police pursuits were initiated for felony crimes. In another study by Alpert and Dunham (1988) it was discovered that, of the suspects who were apprehended upon termination of a pursuit, 48 percent were arrested for a felony.

Police pursuits have also involved the legal system to a large extent. Subsequent chapters will explore the Supreme Court as well as District Courts as they have been called upon to rule on issues such as Fourth Amendment seizure considerations, Fourteenth Amendment due process concerns, and uses of force in pursuits.

The Supreme Court refuses to specifically detail the circumstances under which a pursuit amounts to a Fourth Amendment seizure but suggests that a pursuit "communicate to a reasonable person that he was not at liberty to ignore the police presence and go about his business" (*Michigan v. Chesternut*, 1988, p. 56). Originally, the Court would agree with the District Courts and state that a pursuit alone did not constitute a seizure protected under the Fourth Amendment. Later, a more substantive ruling would be offered when Justice Lamberth stated that, "It is undisputed that the police engaged in a high speed vehicular pursuit of plaintiffs and intended to seize plaintiffs. Under these facts, the court finds that a seizure occurred, invoking the Fourth Amendment's requirements of reasonableness" (*Wright v. District of Columbia*, 1990, p. 9).

Additionally, the Court was called upon to rule on issues related to the Fourteenth Amendment's guarantee of substantive due process. Justices ruled that only arbitrary conduct shocking to the conscience unrelated to the legitimate object of arrest would satisfy the requirements of the Fourteenth Amendment's guarantee of due process.

Thus, it is evident that the area of police vehicular pursuits is replete with many interesting and often conflicting ideas and legal decisions. Many studies have presented pursuits in a context of posing serious safety risks to the general public while other studies have stressed the fact that empirical results indicate pursuits to be relatively safe. Legal rulings, too, have posed fascinating questions for both police administrators as well as academics studying this area of law enforcement. It is the responsibility of police administrators to synthesize the findings of academics with the decision of judges and justices to arrive at the ideal pursuit policy. This would serve the officer, the public, and the department well, as pursuit litigation is destructive to all involved.

As a final note, many departments are currently experimenting with various tactics to reduce (and possibly eliminate) the need for high-speed vehicular pursuits. Aerial pursuit is an ongoing tactic used by many larger urban departments. Aircraft such as helicopters can hover and maneuver in ways that can safely track a perpetrator, whether fleeing on foot or in a vehicle. Safety is always foremost in an administrator's mind and aircraft are an excellent, albeit costly, method of pursuing suspects safely and with minimal danger to the general public. Perhaps the costs saved in decreasing pursuit litigation caused by vehicular pursuits could be put to good use in increased air patrol and pursuit.

Larger metropolitan agencies are also experimenting with "stop" techniques such as "sticky foam," pulse guns, and high-tech road spikes in an effort to decrease the need for vehicular pursuits while continuing to apprehend suspects. The added safety to the general population has been an impetus for departments to increase funding for these new tools used in the apprehension of suspects. While no technological miracle has been developed to safely apprehend fleeing suspects while posing no threat of danger to the officer or general public, many new devices have proven to have a great deal of potential in this regard.

REFERENCES

Alpert, G. P. (1987). Questioning police pursuits in urban areas. *Journal of Police Science and Administration, 15:* 298–306.

Alpert, G., & Dunham, R. (1988). Research on police pursuits: Applications for law enforcement. *American Journal of Police, 7:* 123–131.

Alpert, G., & Fridell, L. (1992). Police vehicles and firearms. Prospect Heights, IL: Waveland Press.

Cole, G., & Smith, C. (2001). The American system of criminal justice (9th ed.). Belmont, CA: Wadsorth.

Eulau, H., & Prewitt, K. (1971). *Labyrinths of democracy.* Indianapolis, IN: Bobbs-Merrill, Co.

Heclo, H. H. (1972). Policy analysis. *British Journal of Political Science, 2*(1): 83–108.

International Association of Chiefs of Police (1995). *Pursuit policy.* Washington D.C.: U.S. National Highway Traffic Safety Administration.

Kenney, J. P. (1972). *Police administration.* Springfield, IL: Charles C Thomas.

Marx, F. M. (1963). *Elements of public administration* (2nd ed.). Englewood Cliffs, NJ: Prentice-Hall.

Michigan v. Chesternut, 486 U.S. 567, 569 (1988).

Nicolaidis, N. G., & Donner, J. W. (1960). *Fund publication no. II.* School of Public Administration, University of Southern California.

Payne, D. (1993). *Preliminary findings from the Michigan emergency response study: Phase III. A report to the Michigan State Police training division.* East Lansing, MI: Michigan State University.

Payne, D. M. (1997). Michigan Emergency Response Study–Phase III: Implications of the failure to report pursuits and inaccurate accident reporting: A research note. *Policing: An International Journal of Police Strategy and Management, 20*(2): 256–269.

Peters, B. G. (1982). *American public policy: Processes and performance.* New York: Franklin Watts.

Pfiffner, J. M. (1960). *Administrative rationality.* Public Administration Review, 20(3): 127–132.

Rousseau, J. J. (1948). *The social contract.* New York: Oxford University Press.

Urbonya, K. (1987). Establishing a deprivation of a Constitutional right to personal security under Section 1983: The use of unjustified force by state officials in violation of the Fourth, Eight, and Fourteenth Amendments. *Alabama Law Review, 51:* 173.
Wright v. District of Columbia, Memorandum Opinion, No. 87–2157 (June 21, 1990).

Chapter 2

PREVIOUS RESEARCH

The myriad of issues surrounding police pursuits have been sensationalized to the point that the general public has been presented with an inaccurate and highly suspicious picture of pursuits (Barth, 1981). Police officers understand that their actions in many pursuits will be questioned and scrutinized by administrators as well as scholars researching the issues surrounding their decisions. Debate concerning the viability of a national pursuit policy has generated much controversy as speculation and pseudoscience have been used by the unscrupulous in efforts to portray pursuits as highly dangerous and in need of new administrative policy. It is interesting to note that past researchers have debated, in an academic forum, the merits of police pursuits for years. Many studies have found, and continue to discover, that pursuits are not as dangerous as previously considered. The rates of accidents, injuries, and fatalities have been found to be similar in many research endeavors across the nation. No discussion of police pursuits would be complete without a thorough examination of prior scholarly research into the area.

Early research into police pursuits was, at times, sensational, not likening itself to the scientific structure of modern academic projects. Later it was discovered that some studies of police pursuits were to be of limited scholarly value. It became difficult, if not impossible to make generalizations based upon many of these early investigations (Fennessy, Hamilton, Joscelyn, & Merritt, 1970; Physicians for Automotive Safety, 1968; Beckman, 1983). While these studies contributed to the overall store of knowledge pertaining to pursuits, methodological differences, nonetheless, made the study of pursuits difficult if not suspicious.

Vehicular pursuits have progressively grown into a major social problem as pursuit litigation continues to cost taxpayers and individual officers millions of dollars annually (Alpert & Fridell, 1992). In addition, there remains some threat to the safety of the officers and the general public associated with many pursuits. It is up to police administrators to be adept enough at policy development and implementation to maintain the proper function of law enforcement while simultaneously maintaining public safety. In addition, public support for the police function is another factor to be considered in policy development and implementation. Research has demonstrated that public support for pursuits decreases as the severity of the offense effecting the pursuit decrease (Hill, 2002).

While the safety risk is not exorbitantly high, it is nonetheless present. Police officers are charged with protecting the public; placing them in unnecessary risk is counter to established police protocol. Despite the conjecture surrounding the dangerous aspects of police pursuits, there is little doubt that high-speed chases can become dangerous quite quickly in some circumstances. Research has demonstrated that approximately 50 percent of all pursuit accidents occur within the first two minutes of the pursuit, with more than 70 percent of collisions occurring before the sixth minute of pursuit (Alpert, 1998).

Perhaps the most comprehensive study into police pursuits was conducted by Charles, Falcone, and Wells (1992; 1992a). In a study of 51 Illinois police departments, researchers conducted an administrative survey, a police field interview form, an administrative telephone survey, and an officer survey. Officers reported 875 police pursuits, indicating an accident rate of 34 percent (n = 298), an injury rate of 17 percent (n = 149), a fatality rate of 1.7 percent (n = 15), and a property damage rate of 34 percent (n = 298) (Charles, Falcone, & Wells, 1992).

In addition, Charles, Falcone, and Wells (1992) reported that 16 percent of the accidents involved third parties. Pursuit-related injuries occurred in only 9 percent of the pursuits and injuries to officers and innocent third parties were even less frequent. While the National Highway Traffic Safety Administration (NHTSA) reported 314 fatalities resulting from police pursuits for the year 1990, Charles et al. believed this to be an underestimation. This was based partially on other figures provided by the NHTSA, which included an estimation of 20,000 injuries occurring annually from over 50,000 pursuits (Britz

& Payne, 1994).

Results from the work of Charles, Falcone, and Wells also indicated that 95.9 percent of all officers voiced approval for pursuits and 62 percent reported that felony offenses were more likely to instigate a high-speed chase. Officers also indicated that their approval or tolerance for a pursuit increased in proportionality to the seriousness of the crime. When asked about the possibility of the abolishment of pursuits, officers believed that the police as a law enforcement institution would suffer a loss of respect from the general public as well as potential offenders. As observed by Britz and Payne (1994), "An overwhelming majority of respondents (96%) supported the notion that more offenders would attempt to elude police if such a policy were implemented" (p. 117). In addition, 76.3 percent of officers indicated that they believed the danger to the public would increase and 85.4 percent maintained that crime in general would increase (Charles et al., 1992a).

While many studies have provided consistent findings, some endeavors have contributed contradictory results and analyses. One noteworthy example of such confusing and contradictory results is that of the 1968 study conducted by the Physicians for Automotive Safety (PAS). The PAS, by relying on three months of newspaper clippings, estimated that 20 percent of all police pursuits resulted in fatalities, while 70 percent ended in accidents. Charles and Falcone (1992) later reported that the PAS study was fraught with methodological flaws and was an example of a policy-related study with questionable research procedures, poor reporting, and questionable results. Despite its many imperfections, the PAS study continues to be utilized by attorneys in litigation against the police in pursuit related suits.

The PAS data were later contradicted in a study conducted by the California Highway Patrol (CHP)(1983) that conducted a six-month investigation of all CHP pursuits and those of ten cooperating law enforcement agencies in southern California. The findings collected on the 683 pursuits contradicted earlier studies with the observation that only 1 percent (n = 7) of all pursuits ended in a fatality with 29 percent (n = 198) resulting in accidents, and only 11 percent (n = 75) resulting in injury of any kind (CHP, 1983). Thus, results indicated that the typical law enforcement pursuit did not result in death or injury to innocent persons and injury to third parties was quite rare.

Alpert and Dunham (1988) used a modified version of the CHP

instrument in a study of the Metro Dade Police Department and the Miami Police Department. In an analysis of 952 pursuits, results indicated that 31 percent (n = 298) of the suspects escaped, while 68 percent (n = 646) were apprehended and arrested. Of the suspects who were apprehended, 47 percent (n = 305) were arrested for traffic violations and 48 percent (n = 314) were arrested for felonies. Alpert and Dunham also found that 33 percent (n = 314) of the reported pursuits involved accidents, 17 percent (n = 161) involved injuries, and 0.7 percent (n = 7) resulted in a fatality. The researchers would later conclude that their analysis of the pursuits failed to provide support for a contention that police pursuits resulted in an unfavorable cost-benefit ratio.

In another recent study of police pursuits in Michigan, Payne (1993) reported that the majority of pursuits were initiated for speeding (30.5%), followed by other traffic violations (24.9%) and suspected felony crimes (24.3%). Upon apprehension of the suspect, Payne found that 34.5 percent of the pursuits resulted in an arrest involving a felony, 33.1 percent involved a charge of fleeing and eluding with 14.4 percent involving drunk driving charges. Payne also found that accidents occurred in 67 out of 197 police pursuits amounting to an accident ratio of 34 percent.

In a study conducted by Crew and Hart (1999), data were collected over a nine-year period in the state of Minnesota. Data demonstrated an accident rate of 25.5 percent, an injury rate of 15.8 percent, and a fatality rate of 0.2 percent. It should be noted that the definition of the occurrence of an accident in the Crew and Hart study included any minor automobile damage as well as major collisions between any nearby automobiles; thus, at least a partial explanation for the dramatic differences in accident rates. This study serves to demonstrate the many varied results obtained in studies relating to police pursuits.

In a recent study by the city of Chicago, it was observed that the Chicago Police Department conducted 625 pursuits in the year 2002, resulting in 41 wrecked police squad cars, and 113 civilian crashes (Crime Control Digest, 2003). Due to the City Council's proposal to implement restrictions on police pursuits, the department developed a new written policy to aid officers in instances of high-speed pursuit. This policy prohibits pursuits for most routine traffic violations and places tighter controls on officers in unmarked vehicles. The more restrictive policy is designed to increase police accountability and pub-

lic safety while simultaneously reducing the dangerousness of vehicular pursuits.

Beckman (1986), in his Michigan State University study, also utilizing a modified version of the CHP questionnaire, surveyed nine states
and two U.S. territories over the course of a five-month investigation.
Results indicated an accident rate of 42 percent (n = 178), injury rate
of 14 percent (n = 59), and a fatality rate of only 2.9 percent (n = 12).
What was absent from the researcher's explanation of the methodology was a comprehensive explanation of how officers were sampled
and surveyed for the study. It is still not clear whether officers completed the survey forms immediately prior to a pursuit or after the fact
at some different locale. It is also not clear if all officers of a specific
agency were surveyed or if a sample of officers was chosen to complete surveys. Although the researcher failed to provide many details
pertinent to his project, the data, nonetheless, proved to be quite use-
ful for a general understanding of accident, injury, and fatality rates
associated with police pursuits.

In another study, Auten (1991) used a survey instrument in his study
of 86 police agencies in Illinois. In an effort to make the results more
generalizeable and less skewed, the researcher omitted the state police
and the Chicago police, the state's two largest departments. Results
indicated an accident rate of 41 percent (n = 118), an injury rate of 12
percent (n = 34), and a fatality rate of 1.4 percent (n = 4). Auten cau-
tioned against attempts to generalize his data to the entire state. Such
generalizations must be done with caution, as Illinois is large with vastly differing demographics across sections of the state.

In a study of a more rural nature, Oechsli (1990) worked with the
Kentucky State Police, collecting data on intra-agency teletypes. While
details on the exact methodology used by Oechsli and the State Police
were not provided, results, nevertheless, served to bolster arguments
that police pursuits were safer than some had posited previously.
Results indicated a total of 235 pursuits with an accident rate of 29 percent (n = 178), an injury rate of 5 percent (n = 37), and a fatality rate
of 0.4 percent (n = 1).

In a limited project, Fennessy, Hamilton, Joscelyn, and Merritt
(1970) worked with the North Carolina Department of Motor Vehicles
in a six-day study of the Departmental offices in response to claims
made by the Physicians for Automotive Safety (PAS) (1968). The survey of the offices indicated a total of 44 pursuits with an accident rate

of 11 percent (n = 5), an injury rate of 4 percent (n = 2), and a fatality rate of 0 percent (n = 0). The researchers themselves reported crucial methodological flaws in the study pointing to the small sample, inadequate questionnaire training, and short duration of the study (November 4, 1968 to November 10, 1968).

Finally, in a 1986 study, Patinkin and Bingham worked with the Chicago Police Department in an examination of local pursuits. Results indicated a total of 741 pursuits with an accident rate of 24 percent (n = 178), an injury rate of 5 percent (n = 37), and a fatality rate of 1 percent (n = 7).

The results of the many previous research endeavors into the field of pursuit are summarized in Table 2.1. It can be seen by this table that of the many studies into police pursuits there is a great deal of disparity between studies as to the numbers of accidents, injuries, fatalities, and property damage.

Data from the National Highway Traffic Safety Administration (NHTSA) and the Fatality Analysis Reporting Systems (FARS) were utilized in an effort to come to terms with the disparity observed among previous research concerning the precise number of fatalities occurring as a result of police pursuits. As can be surmised by Table 2.1, there is considerable discrepancies between many research endeavors and official data as to the exact number of individuals killed or injured as a result of police pursuits. Table 2.2 depicts the results of the NHTSA and FARS concerning the rates of fatalities occurring as a direct result of police vehicular pursuits. Although the numbers observed in Table 2.2 might initially appear quite large, it is necessary to take into consideration the reporting practices of the average law enforcement officer (2003).

In addition to the perceived danger posed by pursuits, the failure of officers to report instances of high-speed chases has repeatedly alarmed researchers and scholars. Charles, Falcone, and Wells (1992), Payne and Corley (1994), and Falcone (1994) have noted the existences of a shocking trend in underreporting of police pursuits. There has emerged a dramatic disparity between the official record of pursuits and those in which officers actually engage. It has been estimated that the failure to report vehicular pursuits might be as high as a factor of 14.5 (Payne, 1997). Thus is borne the "dark figure" of pursuits.

Table 2.1
SUMMARY OF INJURIES, ACCIDENTS, FATALITIES, AND PROPERTY DAMAGE
RESULTING FROM VEHICULAR PURSUITS ACROSS THE UNITED STATES.

Source	Accident Rate		Injury Rate		Fatality Rate		Property Damage		Pursuits
	%	N	%	N	%	N	%	N	N
MERS (Payne, 1997)	33	65	16.2	32	0.5	1	16.25	32	197
N. Carolina (Fennessy, Hamilton, Joscelyn, & Merritt, 1970)	11	5	4	2	0	0	7	3	44
Michigan State University (Beckman, 1986)	42	178	14	59	2.9	12	25	106	424
California Highway Patrol (1983)	29	198	11	75	1	7	29	198	683
Charles, Falcone, & Wells (1992)	34	298	17	149	1.7	15	34	298	875
Illinois (Auten, 1991)	41	118	12	34	1.4	4	28	80	286
Miami/Dade (Alpert & Dunham, 1988)	33	314	17	161	0.7	7	15.3	146	959
Kentucky State Police (Oechsli, 1990)	29	68	5.6	13	0.4	1	23	54	235
Chicago Police Department (Patinkin & Bingham, 1986)	24	178	5	37	1	7	18	133	741

Table 2.2
YEARLY FATALITIES OCCURRING AS A
RESULT OF POLICE VEHICULAR PURSUITS.

Year	Pursuing Officer	Suspect	Other Motorists	Bystanders	Total
	Nature of Fatality				
1992	1	224	66	7	298
1993	1	284	57	5	347
1994	3	284	93	12	392
1995	10	249	117	10	386
1996	5	267	109	9	390
1997	1	193	100	11	305
1998	2	201	105	14	322
1999	3	212	99	5	319
2000	7	185	103	10	305
2001	4	221	119	21	365

LEGAL ASPECTS

The field of police vehicular pursuits is replete with complex, often conflicting, legal issues. The consequences of negligence can have far-reaching implications for law enforcement agencies as well as individual officers. Litigation can be financially devastating for a department. The need for comprehensive pursuit policy is never so evident as in a brief synopsis of the many recent pursuit legal decisions. Administrators and policymakers need to continually update policy so as to effect any revisions necessary to take into consideration recent court rulings. While this is not an appropriate venue for an in-depth legal analysis of pursuit ramifications, the synopsis below will provide the discriminating reader with a guide to understanding the many legal intricacies involved in police pursuits.

FOURTH AMENDMENT

It has been argued that the ultimate issue concerning police pursuit rests on the Fourth Amendment question of whether the police 'seize' a suspect by initiating a pursuit (Alpert & Fridell, 1992). The Fourth Amendment ensures, "The right of the people to be secure in their persons, houses, papers, and effects, against unreasonable searches and seizures, shall not be violated, and no warrant shall issue, but upon probable cause, supported by oath or affirmation, and particularly describing the place to be searched, and the persons or things to be seized."

A number of lower courts have interpreted the ruling in *Brower v. County of Inyo* (1989) to indicate that a seizure under the Fourth Amendment does not occur when a police officer initiates a pursuit of a suspect. It was understood that a seizure under the Fourth Amendment does not occur, ". . . whenever there is a governmentally caused termination or governmentally desired termination of an individual's freedom of movement . . . , but only where there is a governmental termination of freedom of movement through means intentionally applied" (*Brower v. County of Inyo,* 1989, p. 1381). Thus, the court interpreted this ruling to indicate that a pursuit is not in fact a seizure applicable under the Fourth Amendment.

The issue of a suspect's Fourth Amendment rights had been considered when United States District Court Judge Lamberth relied upon the Supreme Court's decision in *Michigan v. Chesternut* (1988) for the ruling in *Wright v. District of Columbia* (1990) when he stated, "The reasonableness of a seizure is to be assessed by balancing the right of the individual to be free from unreasonable intrusions against the needs of the state to carry out its law enforcement function" (p. 10).

An exception to the position of Justices Kennedy and Scalia would surface in Judge Lamberth's ruling in *Wright v. District of Columbia* (1990) when he stated that, "It is undisputed that the police engaged in a high speed vehicular pursuit of plaintiffs and intended to seize plaintiffs. Under these facts, the court finds that a seizure occurred, invoking the Fourth Amendment's requirements of reasonableness" (p. 9). Thus, it can be argued that the processes involved in police pursuit driving have been identified as a seizure by the Wright Court and when found unreasonable, lends itself to consideration as an issue of liability.

42 U.S.C. § 1983

Any infraction of an individual's civil rights, including police use of force, is litigated under 42 U.S.C. § 1983. In *Baker v. McCollan* (1979), the court decided that the initial inquiry into any § 1983 suit must isolate and identify the constitutional violation before any subsequent action can begin. As previously noted, most pursuit cases will involve some issues relevant to the Fourth Amendment's prohibition against unreasonable searches and seizures.

Title 42 of the United States Code reads, "Every person who, under color of any statute, ordinance, regulation, custom, or usage, of any State or Territory or the District of Columbia, subjects, or causes to be subjected, any citizen of the United States or other persons within the jurisdiction thereof to the deprivation of any rights, privileges, or immunities secured by the Constitution and laws, shall be liable to the party injured in an action at law, suit in equity, or other proper proceeding for redress. For the purposes of this section, any Act of Congress applicable exclusively to the District of Columbia shall be considered to be a statute of the District of Columbia" (p. 1).

The Brower Court (1989) recognized some similarities between the use of a firearm and a police pursuit when it was stated that, "Brower's independent decision to continue the chase can no more eliminate respondent's responsibility for the termination of his movement effected by the roadblock than Garner's independent decision to flee eliminated the Memphis police officer's responsibility for the termination of his movement effected by the bullet" (p. 1381). The Court has relied upon its ruling in *Graham v. Connor* (1989) to assist in a determination of reasonableness when an officer effects a pursuit. The reasonableness of the use of deadly force is determined by analyzing "the severity of the crime at issue, whether the suspect poses an immediate threat to the safety of the officers or others, whether he is actively resisting arrest or attempting to evade arrest by flight" (p. 9).

However, the Court, in *Graham v. Connor* (1989), maintained that, "all claims that law enforcement officers have used excessive force–deadly or not–in the course of arrest, investigatory stop, or other 'seizure' of a free citizen should be analyzed under the Fourth Amendment and its 'reasonableness' standard" (p. 8). In addition, the Court stated in *Terry v. Ohio* (1968) that a seizure, which establishes the Fourth Amendment's protections, occurs only when the police have "by means of physical force or show of authority . . . in some way restrained the liberty of a citizen" (p. 19). Thus, the opportunity for an examination of police pursuit as a Fourth Amendment issue has existed for many years.

The status of police pursuits as subject to Fourth Amendment standards is still hotly debated within the ranks of the legal profession. The District of Columbia, in *Wright v. District of Columbia* (1990), held that a police pursuit constitutes a seizure of the suspect and is, therefore, subject to the Fourth Amendment's standards of reasonableness and probable cause. However, the Sixth Circuit Court in *Galas v. McGee* (1986), remained dubious when it stated that, "without question high-speed pursuit places the suspect, the officer, and the public in general at risk of death or serious bodily injury. In that respect high-speed pursuits are no different than the use of a firearm to apprehend fleeing suspects. We conclude that the minimal intrusion on a traffic offender's Fourth Amendment rights occasioned by the officer's participation in a high-speed pursuit does not outweigh a longstanding police practice which we consider essential to a coherent scheme of powers. Accordingly, we hold that the use of high-speed pursuits to apprehend traffic violators is not unreasonable, and, thus, not violative of the Fourth Amendment" (p. 4).

POLICY CONSIDERATIONS

The field of vehicular pursuits abounds with many important topics of which police administrators must be constantly aware. Researchers continue to develop new, more effective tools, the use of which only serves to strengthen police pursuit policies and protect agencies and officers alike from claims of negligence and liability. Policymakers and administrators must first understand the issues behind claims of liability and negligence as well as the basis behind fundamental policy development. Once the basic building blocks of policy development are understood and appreciated, departmental pursuit policies will offer more protection to civilians, officers, and the agency as a whole.

Emergency vehicles, among which are included police squad cars, are afforded certain privileges exempting them from traffic laws during the performance of law enforcement duties. The ability to refrain from obeying traffic laws related to speed, traffic signals, and right of way poses several dilemmas for police administrators. Therefore, many states have borrowed language from the Uniform Vehicle Code for assistance with the creation of departmental pursuit policies. The Uniform Vehicle Code states that a driver of an emergency vehicle is not relieved "from the duty to drive with due regard for the safety of all persons using the highway, nor protect him from the consequences of an arbitrary exercise of the privileges granted under the exemption" (National Committee on Uniform Traffic Laws and Ordinances, 1967, p. 106). Although the driver of an emergency vehicle is exempt from obeying traffic laws while in the course of professional duties, an officer is, nonetheless, held to a higher standard than a citizen due to their special status within the community.

This special status has come under fire in several noteworthy legal cases. In *Thornton v. Shore* (1983), the Kansas University Police Department was sued by plaintiffs arguing that the officer in question failed to drive with due regard after the deaths of two innocent motorists. Plaintiffs maintained that due to the reckless nature of the suspect being pursued, the officer should have terminated the pursuit based on the foreseeability of an accident or injury. The defending officer maintained that he was immune from liability "pursuant to the state law permitting him to disregard certain traffic laws but not to disregard the duty to drive with due regard for the safety of all persons" (Alpert & Fridell, 1992, p. 22). The court ruled the officer's driving to be reasonable and in accord with the clause of due regard for the safety of citizens.

Chambers v. Ideal Pure Milk Company (1952)

In *Chambers v. Ideal Pure Milk Company*, the Court (1952) stated, "Charged as they were with the obligation to enforce the law, the traffic laws included, they (the police) would have been derelict in their duty had they not pursued him. The police were performing their duty when Shearer, in gross violation of his duty to obey the speed laws, crashed into the milk wagon. To argue that the officers' pursuit caused Shearer to speed may be factually true, but it does not follow that the officers are liable at law for the results of Shearer's negligent speed. Police, cannot be made insurers of the conduct of the culprits they chase" (1952, p. 590).

Even as early as 1952, the special status afforded police emergency vehicles had become a source for litigants seeking compensation from police agencies. The ruling of Chambers set the precedent whereby the police were not held liable for the actions of the defendant during the course of a pursuit. The police would have been considered derelict in their obligation to the general public had they not chosen to pursue the law violator. There are times when pursuit is the only means available by which to apprehend a law violator.

West Virginia v. Fidelity Gas & Casualty Company of New York (1967)

The case of *West Virginia v. Fidelity Gas & Casualty Company of New York* (1967) is significant due to the fact that the court's original decision is on the brink of a reformulation. Originally, the court maintained that, "We are not prepared to hold an officer liable for damages inflicted by the driver of a stolen vehicle whom he was lawfully attempting to apprehend for the fortuitous reason only that the criminal drove through an urban area. To do so would open the door for every desperado to seek sanctuary in the congested confines of our municipalities, serene in the knowledge that an officer would not likely give chase for fear of being liable for the pursued recklessness. Such now is not the law nor should it be the law" (1967, p. 90).

This sentiment, however, is on the cusp of a major transformation in the contemporary views of the courts. In the dissenting opinion of Thornton, Justice Herd stated that, "Even with the [emergency] warnings, however, the driver must operate the [police] vehicle with due regard for the safety of all persons. The majority holds whenever a high speed chase results in a collision between the person pursued and a third party, the pursuing officer has, as a matter of law, met the 'due regard' standard . . . by merely turning on his warning signals. . . . There are numerous scenarios where an accident is caused by one not a party to a collision. It is a question of causation" (*Thornton v. Shore,* 1983, p. 668).

Dissenting opinions such as that of Justice Herd demonstrate just one of the many issues facing police administrators and policymakers as they attempt to solve the intricacies inherent in policy development. While it is not possible, or even wise, to attempt to second guess the decisions of legal professionals in rulings pertaining to liability and negligence claims arising from police pursuits, administrators can be aware of the legal risks imposed whenever an officer pursues a lawbreaker.

Legal issues aside, there is a definite need for adequate policy relating to vehicular pursuits. Officers' discretion and performance must be properly guided before they can become efficient and effective law enforcers. Not only is a policy designed as legal protection for the agency, but officer development and the protection of the general public must also be under consideration as administrators outline a pursuit policy. As stated by James Fyfe (1979), there is a need for written departmental policy, "To do otherwise is to simply leave employees 'in the dark' in the expectation that they will intuitively divine the proper and expected course of action in the performance of their duties. . . . Discretion must be reasonably exercised within the parameters of the expectations of the community, the courts, the legislature and the organization, itself" (p. 1).

CONCLUSION

As iterated in the opening paragraphs of this chapter, there have been numerous efforts to arrive at quantitative data demonstrating pursuits to be more or less dangerous. Due to methodological variation, studies continue to obtain contradictory and confusing results. In addition, officers have repeatedly voiced approval for pursuits stating that they are an important and integral part of law enforcement's efforts to apprehend and bring to justice suspected violators of the law. The one constant in all pursuit research continues to be the necessity for comprehensive and effective policy. Administrators must constantly be aware of recent court rulings on pursuit litigation. Updated, effective policy can protect the department, officer, and public from risks involved with negligence, liability, and needless danger.

Beginning with the study by the Physician's for Automotive Safety (PAS), which found an accident rate of 70 percent and a fatality rate of 20 percent, researchers have endeavored to bring the true nature of danger in police pursuits to the forefront. Despite methodological and jurisdictional variations, researchers have consistently demonstrated pursuits to be less dangerous than originally believed. Accident rates have consistently been found to be below the previous level observed by the PAS. Researchers have found accident rates to vary between a low of 11 percent, found by Fennessy, Hamilton, Joscelyn, and Merritt (1970), to a high of 29 percent discovered by Oechsli (1990).

In addition, fatality rates have been demonstrated to range from a low of 0 percent in one study of the North Carolina Department of Motor Vehicles (Fennessy, Hamilton, Joscelyn, & Merritt, 1970) to a high of 2 percent in a study by Beckman at Michigan State University (1986). Some variation has also been noticed in the rates of injuries observed by researchers. Fennessy, Hamilton, Joscelyn, and Merritt (1970) discovered an injury rate of 4 percent while Charles, Falcone, and Wells (1992) observed an injury rate of 17 percent.

Despite the variation in rates of accidents, injuries, and fatalities, police pursuits, nonetheless, have been identified and supported by researchers and officers, alike, as a necessary and integral component of police work. Routine vehicular pursuits serve to apprehend numerous wanted felons and dangerous suspects. In a study by Payne (1993), it was observed that 24.3 percent of police pursuits were initiated for felony crimes. In another study by Alpert and Dunham (1988), it was discovered that, of the suspects who were apprehended upon termination of a pursuit, 48 percent were arrested for a felony.

Police pursuits have also involved the legal system to a large extent. The Supreme Court as well as District Courts have been called upon to rule on issues such as Fourth Amendment seizure considerations, Fourteenth Amendment due process concerns, and uses of force in pursuits.

The Supreme Court refuses to specifically detail the circumstances under which a pursuit amounts to a Fourth Amendment seizure but suggests that a pursuit "communicate to a reasonable person that he was not at liberty to ignore the police presence and go about his business" (*Michigan v. Chesternut*, 1988, p. 56). Originally, the Court would agree with the District Courts and state that a pursuit alone did not constitute a seizure protected under the Fourth Amendment. Later, a more substantive ruling would be offered when Justice Lamberth stated that, "It is undisputed that the police engaged in a high speed vehicular pursuit of plaintiffs and intended to seize plaintiffs. Under these facts, the court finds that a seizure occurred, invoking the Fourth Amendment's requirements of reasonableness" (*Wright v. District of Columbia*, 1990, p. 9).

Additionally, the Court was called upon to rule on issues related to the Fourteenth Amendment's guarantee of substantive due process. Justices ruled that only arbitrary conduct shocking to the conscience unrelated to the legitimate object of arrest would satisfy the requirements of the Fourteenth Amendments guarantee of due process.

Thus, it is evident that the area of police vehicular pursuits is replete with many interesting and often conflicting ideas and legal decisions. Many studies have presented pursuits in a context of posing serious safety risks to the general public, while other studies have stressed the fact that empirical results indicate pursuits to be relatively safe. Legal rulings, too, have posed fascinating questions for both police administrators as well as academics studying this area of law enforcement. It is the responsibility of police administrators to synthesize the findings of academics with the decision of judges and justices to arrive at the ideal pursuit policy. This would serve the officers, the public, and the department well as pursuit litigation is destructive to all involved.

REFERENCES

Alpert, G., & Dunham, R. (1988). Research on police pursuits: Applications for law enforcement. *American Journal of Police, 7:* 123–131.

Alpert, G., & Fridell, L. (1992). *Police vehicles and firearms.* Prospect Heights, IL: Waveland Press.

Alpert, G. P. (1998). *Pursuit Management Task Force report.* U.S. Department of Justice. National Institute of Justice: Washington, D.C.

Auten, J. (1991). *Police pursuit driving in Illinois: 1990.* Champaign, IL: University of Illinois.

Baker v. McCollan, 443 U.S. 137 (1979).

Barth, L. (1981). Police pursuit: A panopoly of problems. *The Police Chief,* February: 54–55.

Beckman, E. (1983). High speed chases: In pursuit of a balanced policy. *The Police Chief,* January: 34–37.

Beckman, E. (1986). Pursuit driving: A report to law enforcement on factors in police pursuits. *Michigan Police Chiefs Newsletter,* May 26: 34.

Britz, M., & Payne, D. (1994). Policy implications for law enforcement pursuit driving. *American Journal of Police, 13*(1): 113–142.

Brower v. County of Inyo, 489 U.S. 593 (1989).

California Highway Patrol (1983). *Pursuit study.* Sacramento, CA: California Highway Patrol.

Chambers v. Ideal Pure Milk Co. 245 S.W. 2d 589 (Ky. 1952).

Charles, M., Falcone, D., & Wells, E. (1992). *Police pursuit: In pursuit of policy: The policy issue, legal and literature review, and an empirical study* (Vol. 1). Washington, D.C.: AAA Foundation for Traffic Safety.

Charles, M., Falcone, D., & Wells, E. (1992a). *Police pursuit in pursuit of policy: The pursuit issue, legal and literature review, and an empirical study.* Washington, D.C.: AAA Foundation for Traffic Safety.

Charles, M., & Falcone, D. (1992). Illinois' police officer's opinions on police pursuit issues. *American Journal of Police, 11*(3): 69–88.

Crew, R. E., & Hart, R. A. (1999). Assessing the value of police pursuits. *Policing: An International Journal of Police Strategies & Management, 22*(1): 58–73.

Anonymous. (2003). Chicago adopts new policies for pursuit. *Crime Control Digest, 37*(16): 5. Washington, D.C.

Falcone, D. N. (1994). Police pursuits and officer attitudes: Myths and realities. *American Journal of Police, 13*(4): 143–155.

Fennessy, E., Hamilton, T., Joscelyn, K., & Merritt, J. (1970). *A study of the problem of hot pursuit by the police.* Hartford, CT: The Center for the Environment and Man, Inc.

Fyfe, J. (1979). Administrative interventions on police shooting discretion: An empirical examination. *Journal of Criminal Justice, 7:* 309–323.

42 U.S.C. 1983.

Galas v. McGee, 801 F.2d 200 (6th Cir. 1986).

Graham v. Connor, 490 U.S. 386 (1989).

Hill, J. (2002). High-speed police pursuits: Dangers, dynamics, and risk reduction. *FBI Law Enforcement Bulletin, 71*(7): 14–19.

Michigan v. Chesternut, 486 U.S. 567, 569 (1988).

National Committee on Uniform Traffic Laws and Ordinances (1967). *Uniform vehicle code: Rules of the road with statutory annotation, 1967.* Washington, D.C.: National Committee on Uniform Traffic Laws and Ordinances.

National Highway Traffic Safety Administration (2003). *Yearly fatalities occurring as a result of police vehicular pursuits (1992–2001).* National Highway Traffic Safety Administration–Fatality Analysis Reporting Systems (1992–2001). Washington D.C.: NHTSA.

Oechsli, S. (1990). *Kentucky State Police pursuit study 1989–1990.* Rockville, MD: National Institute of Justice.

Patinkin, H. P., & Bingham, H. (1986). Police motor vehicle pursuits: The Chicago experience. *The Police Chief, 53*(7): 61–62.

Payne, D. (1993). *Preliminary findings from the Michigan emergency response study: Phase III. A report to the Michigan State Police training division.* East Lansing, MI: Michigan State University.

Payne, D. M. (1997). Michigan Emergency Response Study–Phase III: Implications of the failure to report pursuits and inaccurate accident reporting: A research note. *Policing: An International Journal of Police Strategy and Management, 20*(2): 256–269.

Payne, D. M., & Corley, C. (1994). Police pursuits: Correlates of the failure to report. *American Journal of Police, 13*(4): 47–72.

Physicians for Automotive Safety (1968). *Rapid pursuit by the police: Causes, hazards, consequences: A national pattern is evident.* New York: Physicians for Automotive Safety.

Terry v. Ohio, 392 U.S. 1 (1968).

Thornton v. Shore, 666 P.2d 655 (Kan. 1983).

West Virginia v. Fidelity Gas & Casualty Co. of N.Y., 263 F. Supp. 88 (D.W.Va. 1967).

Wright v. District of Columbia, Memorandum Opinion, No. 87–2157 (June 21, 1990).

Chapter 3

LIABILITY AND NEGLIGENCE

There exists an exceedingly complex relationship between police pursuits, the use of force, and the realm of policy with which administrators strive to contend. Policymakers rarely witness the barrage of daily tensions experienced by patrol officers as they enforce traffic laws, quell domestic disputes, or help a lost child. Policymakers and administrators alike must be fully aware of the often tense atmosphere within patrol officers worn on a daily basis. In efforts to draft effective and efficient policy, administrators are responsible for a vast array of liability issues and departmental training conceptualizations. There is no single best method through which to incorporate policy into the daily business of a department. It is the responsibility of policymakers and administrators to generate methods by which officers can effectively learn and implement policy in their daily interactions with the civilian population.

The operation of vehicles by the police can be classified into two distinct categories: routine and emergency operations. Police officers are required to operate vehicles during the performance of their daily duties. An officer operating a vehicle under normal, routine conditions is held to the same standard of reasonableness required of the general public. Under routine conditions, any accident or injury incurred during the performance of patrol duties is litigated under the general theory of negligence (Kappeler, 1993). If a violation of law is to be considered negligent, the complainant must demonstrate that the law was designed to prevent the damage or injury inflicted. In addition, the law must have been designed to protect a specific class of persons (Kappeler, 1993).

The second type of operation of vehicles by police officers involves emergency situations. Due to the inherent dangers posed by the use of emergency vehicles in responses by police, all states have enacted statutes governing the operation of emergency vehicles (Silver, 1991). Many jurisdictions grant emergency vehicles limited statutory immunity for any violations of state or municipal traffic regulation incurred during an emergency response (Kappeler, 1993). Thus, police officers are afforded some level of protection while responding to emergency calls for assistance.

Questions have arisen as to what constitutes an emergency situation for police officers. This query is to be determined by the courts based on situational factors and individual officers' perception (Kappeler, 1993). It has been decided by the courts that, basically, an "officer must be involved in emergency use of the vehicle and the officer must reasonably feel that an actual emergency exists" (Kappeler, 1993, p. 99). Previously, the Washington Supreme Court had ruled that, "The test for determining whether a publicly owned vehicle is at a given time responding to an emergency call is not whether an emergency in fact exists at the time but rather whether the vehicle is being used in responding to an emergency call. Whether the vehicle is being so used depends upon the nature of the call that is received and the situation as then perceived to the mind of the driver" (*Lakoduk v. Cruger*, 1956, p. 699).

In some instances, for purposes of immunity, courts hold that the chase or attempted apprehension of a law violator is not always an emergency. Therefore, an officer's negligence in violating traffic regulations is determined by the surrounding circumstances dictating the use of the vehicle and the seriousness of the suspect's behavior (*Fiser v. City of Ann Arbor*, 1983). The Michigan Supreme Court stated that "in order for [statutory immunity] to apply, defendants must show that the officers reasonably believed an emergency existed. The chase or apprehension of violators of the law does not necessarily constitute an emergency situation" (*Fiser v. City of Ann Arbor*, 1983, p. 417).

In states with limited statutory immunity, the officer is not held liable for the violation of a state or municipal traffic regulation while responding to an emergency. A violation of a traffic regulation resulting in injury or damage is not conclusive proof of the officer's negligence (Kappeler, 1993). If a plaintiff should desire to establish proof of negligent operation of an emergency vehicle, factors beyond the mere violation of a traffic law must be established if the claim of negligence is to be supported. Limited statutory immunity varies from state to state and is restricted to the use of vehicles in actual emergency situations.

LIABILITY

One area with which policymakers and administrators must become intimately aware is in the area of liability. Although criminal liability is generally a rarity for the vast majority of police departments, it is, nonetheless, a possibility that must be examined. Under federal law, the most likely criminal liability for improper police conduct would be under Title 18 of U.S. Code Section 242, Criminal Liability for Deprivation of Civil Rights. Another section with which administrators and policymakers should become familiar is Title 18 of the U.S. Code Section 245, Violation of Federally Protected Activities.

Although the federal law has many proclamations against police misconduct, state law has its share of precepts discouraging police indiscretion. Under state law, an officer may be charged with "penal code provisions specifically addressing public officers for offenses such as official oppression or official misconduct" (Carter & Payne, 1988, p. 119). It is also true that an officer could be charged with a standard criminal offense if the officer in question used improper force against a citizen. It is a safe assumption that if an officer were charged with gross misconduct the department and jurisdiction would also be held liable for a civil lawsuit.

There are jurisdictions across the country where police negligence is barred by statutes immunizing officers from liability claims in the emergency operation of vehicles (Kappeler, 1993). Generally these statutes immunize officers from claims of liability when they attempt to apprehend escaping suspects. An example of such a statute was interpreted by the California Supreme Court in the ruling that, "the purpose of the legislation was to immunize public entities and employees from the entire spectrum of potential injuries caused by persons actually or about to be deprived of their freedom who take physical measures of one kind or another to avoid the constraint or escape from it" (*Kisbey v. State of California,* 1984, p. 1096).

While it has been stated that the probability of an officer or department being held criminally liable is not dramatically high, the possibility of a civil suit is, indeed, much higher. Civil lawsuits aimed at police personnel may be based on either state tort law or federal law as found under the Civil Rights Act (Carter & Payne, 1988).

A tort may be defined as, "a wrong, either intentional or unintentional (as when caused by negligence), wherein the action of one person causes injury to the person or property of another in violation of a legal duty imposed by law" (Carter & Payne, 1988, p. 119). If a tort lawsuit is to be brought against an officer or department, it is necessary first that the officer or department act with care toward the suing party. If the duty of the officer was breached and that subsequent breach created the proximate cause of injury to the party as a result, liability may be established. "Injury" in such a case is not limited merely to physical harm, but includes injury to the rights of the person under consideration. There are a myriad of torts for which an officer can be found liable: wrongful death, use of excessive force, invasion of privacy, libel or slander, negligent vehicle operation, or negligent administration of first aid (Siegel, 1989).

The most widely utilized provision of law used in police liability cases is 42 U.S.C. 1983, Deprivation of Civil Rights, a section of the Civil Rights Act of 1964 (Carter & Payne, 1988). Section 1983 of the U.S. penal code states, "Every person who, under color of any statute, ordinance, regulation . . . of any State or Territory . . . causes to be subjected, any citizen of the United states . . . the deprivation of any rights, privileges . . . shall be liable to the party injured in an action at law, in suit in equity, or other proper proceeding for redress" (42 U.S.C. 1983, p. 1). It is necessary to establish officer or department liability under Section 1983 through the presence of four elements: (1) the defendant must be a natural person or a local government; (2) the officer must be acting under color of law; (3) the violation must be of a constitutional or federally protected right; (4) the violation must reach a constitutional level (Carter & Payne, 1988). For an officer or a department to act under color of law, the entity must be acting "with the appearance of legal authority; in actual or purported performance of one's duties as a state official" (Clapp, 1996, p. 274).

Once liability has been established, the plaintiff in a Section 1983 suit may request three types of relief: monetary relief, declaratory relief, or injunctive relief. Monetary relief, on which there is no set limit amount, is awarded when defendants are required to pay the plaintiff for damages incurred as a result of actions of the officer.

Declaratory relief is characterized by a declaration of the court that the officer and/or department acted improperly and bears the full brunt of responsibility for the actions in question. The court grants, in injunctive relief, the plaintiff's request that a change in operations or behavior of the officer and/or department. The impact of injunctive relief cannot be underestimated. The court can mandate policy and managerial operations for which a department has little choice but to follow.

Policymakers must also understand that liability can be both a direct as well as vicarious phenomenon. If an individual is the direct cause of the resultant injury or violation, it is defined by a claim of direct liability. Substituted responsibility, where supervisors, administrators, and others in the hierarchical chain of command are held responsible for the actions of their subordinates, is characteristic of vicarious liability. A plaintiff wishing to establish vicarious liability must demonstrate that the police department acted negligently, or with deliberate indifference, in permitting improper police conduct. Generally, it is necessary for the plaintiff to be required to demonstrate a pattern of misconduct to exist within a department. However, in instances of gross impropriety, it may not be necessary to establish a pattern of behavior.

MUNICIPAL LIABILITY

Municipal liability should be a central concern to administrators and policymakers within a law enforcement organization. Eventually municipalities would be exposed to unprecedented liability by the Supreme Court (*Monroe v. Pape,* 1961). Here, the Court ruled that municipalities were not liable as "persons" under Section 1983 (Hall, 1988). This decision would later be overturned when the Supreme Court concluded that "the legislative history of the act supported a statutory construction that defined 'persons' to include municipalities" (Lewis, 1991, p. 556; *Monell v. Department of Social Services,* 1978). Therefore, the Court determined that a government entity may be held liable under 42 U.S.C. 1983. However, such liability must be found upon evidence "that the government unit itself supported a violation of constitutional rights" and not on the basis of the "respondent superior doctrine or vicarious liability" (Lewis, 1991, p. 556).

Thus, municipal liability applies only when the execution of a government's policy or custom inflicts the subsequent injury. Generally, the presentation of evidence of statutes, official proclamations, or policy directives suffices to establish expressed municipal policy (Lewis, 1991). A single application of an expressed policy deemed unconstitutional is sufficient to invoke court action.

While it might seem a relatively simple task to establish municipal liability through the presentation of statutes, proclamations, and directives, it is quite another to prove a custom a violation of constitutional rights. In response to this question, the Supreme Court ruled that "proof of a single incident of unconstitutional activity is not sufficient to impose liability under Monell, unless proof of the incident includes proof that it was caused by an existing unconstitutional municipal policy that can be attributed to the municipal policymaker" (Lewis, 1991, p. 557; *Oklahoma v. Tuttle,* 1985).

BARRIERS TO LIABILITY

Findings of police liability in some jurisdictions are limited by an adoption of the ministerial/discretionary function distinction (*Johnson v. State of California,* 1987). A ministerial function is any behavior that is considered a line or operational function such as duties an officer must perform as part of daily operations. Discretionary functions, on the other hand, entail policy development or planning tasks such as the introduction of a new drunk driving policy.

The dichotomy of ministerial and discretionary functions has brought some confusion to the courts. Some courts have ruled that the emergency operation of vehicles is a discretionary function. Thus, in such a case, the courts have rejected claims of police liability for negligent operation of emergency vehicles. However, other jurisdictions have concluded that police pursuits are a ministerial function allowing for claims of liability to be imposed (*Gibson v. Pasadena,* 1987). To assuage some of the confusion brought about by the ministerial/discretionary dichotomy, Kappeler and del Carmen (1988) have noted that courts often maintain that an officer's decision to engage in a pursuit is a discretionary function, while operation of the vehicle is ministerial in nature.

In states retaining some vestiges of sovereign immunity such as Virginia, police pursuit is considered conduct within the "scope of official employment and therefore negligence action is barred" (Kappeler, 1993, p. 101). The State of Michigan has a much different position on the issue of police negligence. The position presented in the Michigan Compiled Law Annotated states, "Governmental agencies shall be liable for bodily injury and property damage resulting from the negligent operation by an officer, agent, or employee of the governmental agency, of a motor vehicle of which the governmental agency is owner, as defined in Act No. 300 of the Public Acts of 1949, as amended, being sections 257.1 to 257.923 of the Compiled Laws of 1948" (Michigan Compiled Laws Annotated 691.1405). Courts are increasingly holding officers, departments, and municipal governments liable for their actions as well as those of the suspect.

NEGLIGENCE

As administrators and policymakers become familiar with the concepts and issues surrounding liability, it is necessary to examine the variety of areas within which officers, supervisors, and their departments can create an environment ripe for claims of negligence.

Negligence has been defined as "inadvertent behavior that results in damage or injury" (Kappeler, 1993, p. 23). In negligence tort, a lesser degree of foreseeability of danger is required than in intentional tort. The mental state of the officer in question is not an issue in an application of negligence tort. Inadvertent behavior leading to injury or damage can be a cause to action under negligence tort. The fundamental standard applied in negligence tort actions is whether the "officer's actions created an unreasonable risk to another member of society" (Kappeler, 1993, p. 23).

There are four basic elements needed to establish a case of police negligence: legal duty, a breach of that duty, actual damage or injury to another party, and the proximate cause of such damage due to actions of the officer (Kappeler, 1993). Negligence is generally determined by the facts of the case and the utilization of the reasonableness standard (Payne & Corley, 1994). The task is left to the courts to determine what any reasonable and prudent emergency driver would do in the circumstances surrounding an emergency (*Rutherford v. State*, 1979). Once reasonableness has been determined, it is left to the plaintiff to demonstrate proof of negligence providing evidence showing a

duty to the injured party, a breach of that duty, and an injury proxi-
mately resulting from that breach (*Brooks v. Lundeen,* 1981).

Basically, there are eight areas where an officer, supervisor, or
department can be held responsible for negligence in the fulfillment of
basic duties: negligent hiring, negligent assignment, failure to train,
negligent entrustment, failure to supervise, failure to direct, negligent
retention, and failure to protect. In a case alleging negligent hiring, liability may ensue if it can be established that an employee is unfit for
appointment as a police officer and such unfitness was known by the
department. Negligent hiring can also be established if it can be shown
that the department should have been aware of an employee's unsuitability as an officer (Carter & Payne, 1988).

Negligent assignment refers to the assignment of an officer to a job
or task without ascertaining if the individual was prepared to adequately perform the responsibilities required for the task. Negligent
assignment can also occur when an officer remains in a position for
which incompatibility has been demonstrated (Carter & Payne, 1988).

An allegation of failure to train is a failure of the department to
properly provide a subordinate with the skills, training, knowledge, or
activities required to adequately perform the tasks incumbent of
employment as a police officer.

Negligent entrustment occurs when there is a failure of a supervisor
to properly supervise an officer's custody or use of equipment provided for completion of the duties required of a police officer. It has been
stated that in a case alleging negligent entrustment, it is a "test of deliberate indifference. The plaintiff must be able to prove that the officer
was incompetent, inexperienced, or reckless, and that the supervisor
knew or had reason to know of [the] officer's incompetence" (del
Carmen, 1986, p. 318).

In a case of failure to supervise, it must be shown that a superior officer, at any step along the hierarchy of command, was negligent in the
duty to oversee subordinate performance of official duties in accordance with the law. Liability can be established if a supervisor failed to
enforce organizational policy in a regular manner.

Very similar to failure to train is failure to direct. The police department has the responsibility of instructing its employees in the specific
procedures, conditions, and limits associated with performance of
their respective duties.

Negligent retention occurs when the police department fails to take appropriate disciplinary actions or retraining efforts of an officer who has demonstrated unsuitability for the position as a police officer to a dangerous degree (Swanson, Territo, & Taylor, 1993).

The final area of organizational negligence is failure to protect. A claim of failure to protect asserts that the police failed to take affirmative or preventive measures to protect an individual from injury or harm (Carter & Payne, 1988).

LEGAL DUTY

A legal duty is any behavior recognized by the court requiring police officers to either take appropriate action or to refrain from taking action in certain situations (Kappeler, 1993). The duties required of police officers arise from various sources including law, custom, judicial decisions, and departmental policy. Previously, many plaintiffs were unsuccessful in establishing the fact that this duty was not owed to individuals. However, lately this has begun to change. Many courts now recognize that under certain circumstances, the police may owe a special duty to individual citizens. In such a case, the actions of the police serve to set the individual apart from the general public (Kappeler, 1993).

BREACH OF DUTY AND PROXIMATE CAUSE

The existence of a legal duty of protection is not sufficient in and of itself to establish officer liability in negligence suits. The plaintiff must demonstrate that the officer breached the duty of protection to the citizen (Kappeler, 1993). Courts recognize that the police are only liable to specific individuals and not to the general public as a whole. As noted by Kappeler (1993), "There must exist some special knowledge of circumstances that sets the individual citizen apart from the general public and shows a relationship between that citizen and the police" (p. 25). However, it is important to point out that courts recognize a duty of care by police officers operating emergency vehicles" (Kappeler, 1993). Operators of emergency vehicles are required to drive with "due care for the safety of all persons using the public roadways" (Kappeler, 1993, p. 102).

Once a plaintiff has successfully demonstrated the existence of a police duty and has established the parameters of the breach of that duty to a specific citizen, it is still required that the plaintiff prove that the officer's action was the proximate cause of the injury or damage (Kappeler, 1993). The proximate cause of an injury or damage can be established by determining if the injury or damage would have been sustained were it not for the actions of the officer. If proximate cause can be established, then the officer can be held liable for the damage or injury. The proximate cause requirement of negligence suits is designed to bar liability in instances where damage or injury would have been suffered regardless of the actions of the police.

Courts have utilized two distinct techniques when dealing with issues of proximate cause. The first approach treats cause as a doctrinal barrier to findings of police liability for injuries sustained by third parties in a pursuit (Kappeler, 1993). Courts using this line of reasoning maintain that the conduct of an officer in the midst of a pursuit cannot be the proximate cause for injuries or damage suffered by an innocent third party (Kappeler, 1993). Hence, such courts are reluctant to discover police liability if an officer's vehicle is not directly involved in an accident with the injured party's vehicle. Courts operating under this philosophy do not extend the zone of proximate cause beyond the actual collision of the police vehicle and the third party.

Kappeler (1993) has stated that such reasoning is based on three points:

1. Police officers have a duty to pursue, apprehend, and arrest law violators. The courts deem this duty so important that it outweighs any other policy concern. From this position, the duty of care becomes subordinate to the duty to apprehend.
2. Police officers and public entities should not become the insurers of the negligence damage caused by law violators.
3. The actions of a fleeing law violator are an intervening cause which negates the possibility of an officer's conduct constituting the proximate cause of injury. (p. 111)

The second approach uses the principle of proximate cause as a guide to determine whether specific police conduct is the cause of injury or damage (Kappeler, 1993). This approach also reflects a growing trend among state courts. Courts examine the situational factors surrounding the conduct of the officer in efforts to determine proximate cause. Rather than formulating a blanket pronouncement on proximate cause, courts using this approach adopt a case-by-case method. In utilizing a case-by-case method, courts do not automatically confine proximate cause to the zone of contact between the police vehicle and the injured party. Instead, the conduct of a "pursuing police officer may be the proximate cause of injuries sustained in an accident even where the police vehicle did not directly become involved in the collision" (Kappeler, 1993, p. 102). This frees the court to determine proximate cause and police liability by examining the extent to which the officer's conduct and the situational factors surrounding the accident contributed to the injury or damage.

Similar to the first approach, this judicial approach to proximate cause is based on certain legal principles. Courts have recognized a refusal to recognize an absolute duty to apprehend suspected law violators. Thus, officers cannot utilize any method available in an effort to apprehend a suspected law violator. Care must be taken to protect the lives and property of citizens and bystanders. Second, courts have noted a refusal to relegate the duty of care to the duty to apprehend. Here again, officers must use due care for the safety and well being of innocent bystanders when endeavoring to apprehend an offender. The duty to apprehend an offender is not necessarily more important than the duty of care for the general public.

Third, courts have accepted the possibility of a concurring cause modification of proximate cause doctrine. It has been noted that the cause of an accident might have a secondary causal factor other than that of the officer in pursuit of a suspect. Fourth, higher courts have demonstrated deference to subjective jury decision making. Lower courts have been afforded the opportunity to allow juries to render verdicts in many instances of police liability and negligence. Finally, courts have adopted an application of a failure to warn doctrine (Kappeler, 1993, p. 111). Officers in pursuit of a suspected offender have a duty to warn bystanders of danger while engaged in a pursuit by means of the use of a siren and warning lights.

If a plaintiff is successful in establishing duty of protection, a breach of duty, and proximate cause, it is still necessary to determine if actual injury or damage has been suffered. The plaintiff must demonstrate that the damage or injury was such that it "substantially interfered with an interest of an individual or his/her property" (Kappeler, 1993, p. 26).

BREACH OF REASONABLENESS

Courts have determined that negligence is a question of fact and law that is established by proving the existence of duty and then observing a behavior that constitutes a breach of that duty (Kappeler, 1993). The traditional approach of the courts considering issues of negligence is to develop principles that negate breaches of the reasonableness standard (Kappeler, 1993). In so doing, the courts do not consider every specific action by the officer that may breach a duty. Legal principles developed by the courts exclude certain types of conduct from constituting a breach of duty. Theoretically, this practice provides consistency in judicial decision making.

The principles negating a breach of duty are derived from two legal distinctions. First, courts distinguish between the "actual operation of an emergency vehicle and the initial decision making process of the pursuing officer" (Kappeler, 1993, p. 112). Courts have held that the duty of care standard and reasonableness test are invoked only by the actual operation of the emergency vehicle. The officer's decision to pursue a suspect is not applied to the reasonableness test or the duty of care standard. This, in effect, shields officers from claims of liability associated with their decision-making processes.

The second distinction deals with the physical operation of the police emergency vehicle. In this instance, the court isolates certain types of conduct and removes them from other actions which constitute conclusive proof of officer negligence. The courts have held that an officer exceeding the speed limit in pursuit of a suspect is not an instance of police negligence (*Brown v. City of New Orleans,* 1985; *Riggs v. State,* 1986). The distinction is based on the totality of circumstances, not simply officer decision making.

Under this distinction, a plaintiff is forced to establish that an officer's conduct was a breach of reasonableness (Kappeler, 1993). This can prove to be a daunting task when the totality of circumstances is considered instead of the individual aspects of the pursuit. A single factor such as high speeds or failure to use emergency sirens is not conclusive proof of police negligence. Generally, state courts consider a variety of factors in determining negligence in police pursuit cases. The factors considered by the state courts can be grouped together into four zones of negligence: justifications for pursuits, actual vehicle operation, circumstances of operation, and external factors (Kappeler,

1993).

The first justification courts have taken into consideration has been the presence of a real or apparent emergency (*Hamilton v. Town of Palo,* 1976; *Keating v. Holston's Ambulance Service, Inc.,* 1989). As stated previously, an emergency has been demonstrated if an officer honestly believes an emergency to exist. A second justification considered by the courts pertains to whether the officer's conduct was serious (*Gibson v. Pasadena,* 1978). A serious breach of the reasonableness standard would surely place the officer, as well as the department, in danger of negligence liability. However, reasonable conduct on the part of the officer greatly lessens any threat of liability for the department and the officer in question. Third, the court contemplates whether alternatives to pursuit were available to the officer (*Mason v. Britton,* 1975). If an officer is faced with viable alternatives to a pursuit then claims of negligence can be substantiated. However, the court will recognize if an officer has no option but to pursue an offender. Finally, the court considers whether the apprehension of the suspect was feasible. If apprehension of a suspect is dubious, an officer and the department may face charges of negligence. However, if a suspect is easily apprehended by means of a pursuit, then claims of negligence and liability are not likely to be substantiated.

Factors in the actual physical operation of the vehicle considered by the courts include the speed at which the vehicle was operated, the use of emergency equipment (*Fowler v. North Carolina Department of Crime Control,* 1989), violation of traffic regulations, and disregard of traffic control devices (*Brown v. City of Pinellas Park,* 1990). If any of these factors are blatantly violated with little regard to the safety of citizens' claims of negligence, liability can be confirmed. However, if an officer takes reasonable care in the pursuit of a suspect, a plaintiff is provided less evidence of officer negligence.

Factors in the circumstances of operation considered by the courts include the physical conditions of the roadway, weather conditions (*Bickel v. City of Downey,* 1987), density of traffic (*Brown v. City of Pinellas Park,* 1990), presence of pedestrians, presence of audio or visual warning devices, and area of pursuit (*Brown v. City of Pinellas Park,* 1990). An officer demonstrating due care and regard for the safety of citizens will take each environmental factor into consideration prior to implementing a pursuit. If a pursuing officer can be demonstrated to have rendered due care with respect to considering each factor during the pursuit, claims of liability and negligence are much more difficult for a plaintiff to prove.

External factors considered by the courts include the violation of departmental policy regarding police pursuits, an officer's training in pursuit driving (*West v. United States,* 1985), and the physical and visual condition of the police vehicle. Claims of negligence are much more difficult for a plaintiff to validate if an officer has been trained in pursuit driving by the department and adheres to departmental policy regarding pursuits. The condition of the police vehicle enables a court to determine whether the officer in question drove with reckless abandon in attempts to apprehend the suspected law violator. If a plaintiff can prove any one of these factors, it is a much easier task to support claims of police liability and negligence in court.

DELIBERATE INDIFFERENCE

The area of deliberate indifference poses some interesting problems for policymakers. Officers need to understand instances where suspects might genuinely require medical care. The failure to be sensitive to the personal needs of suspects and prisoners can be a serious issue of liability for officers and department alike.

The Supreme Court has rejected the contention that a municipality can be held liable under Section 1983 only if the policy of the municipality was itself unconstitutional (*Canton v. Harris,* 1989). This ruling required plaintiffs to bridge the gap between policy and injury in a stringent manner. The Court adopted the deliberate indifference standard that was required to be met to establish a constitutional violation by a municipality. Deliberate indifference is utilized by many plaintiffs seeking compensation for instances of police shootings and the use of excessive force. Most of the claims center around a municipality's failure to effectively train its officers so as to avoid the constitutional deprivation (Lewis, 1991).

COURT RULINGS

After administrators and policymakers are adept with the terminology required to understand policy, they must next embark on an endeavor to untangle the intricate web of court rulings relating directly to the use of force by police. It is a basic necessity, when writing effective and efficient policy, to take into consideration the decisions of the courts. It does a department little benefit to write policy with no conscious effort to synthesize the organizational mission, requirements of law, and court rulings. Administrators must be intimately familiar with what is considered improper police conduct by the courts if they are to draft formal policy.

Due to the fact that this is not the proper venue for a detailed legal analysis of all of the many legal intricacies highlighting police pursuits, a matrix has been developed to assist in a brief synopsis of the variety of legal issues placed before the courts. This matrix has been divided into discrete categories detailing operational considerations ruled upon in the court system and administrative aspects on which the courts have ruled. Table 3.1 and Table 3.2 provide the legal matrix of operational/tactical and administrative issues inherent in police pursuits.

RECENT RULINGS

Davis v. Township of Hillside (1999)

The case of Davis v. Township of Hillside (1999), currently before the United States Court of Appeals 3rd Circuit, contends a violation of civil rights by police officers after a fleeing suspect collided with two parked cars, one of which was propelled into the plaintiff, seriously injuring him. In this case, police observed an individual in an automobile acting strangely and driving somewhat erratically. It soon became evident, after checking the license plate number of the automobile, that the suspect was driving a stolen vehicle. After refusing to stop, the suspect led police on a high-speed chase through the streets of the town. Eventually the car spun out of control, hitting two parked cars, one of which was propelled into the plaintiff, resulting in serious injuries. What is interesting about this case concerns the actions of the officers, as they instigated a high-speed chase despite existing regulations to the contrary.

The ruling by the court of appeals affirmed the earlier decision in favor of the defendants, in this case the police. Although the police acted in a way contrary to the established policy of their department, the court, nonetheless, ruled in favor of the police. The decision

Table 3.1
OPERATIONAL/TACTICAL RULINGS OF VARIOUS VEHICULAR PURSUIT CASES.

	Roadblock	Environmental	Traffic Regulations & Conditions	Emergency Equipment	Speed	Existence of Emergency
City of Sacramento v. Superior Court in and for Sacramento County (1982)				X		
Georgia Dept. of Public Safety v. Collins (1977)				X		
Littell v. Maloney (1979)				X		
City of Akron v. Charley (1982)				X		
Semple v. Hope (1984)				X		
Knaggs v. Lewis (1939)						X
Stanulonis v. Marzec (1986)	X					
Brower v. County of Inyo (1987)	X					
Bickel v. City of Downey (1987)		X				
Brown v. City of Pinellas Park (1990)			X			
Brown v. City of New Orleans (1985)					X	
Riggs v. State (1986)					X	
Hamilton v. Town of Palo (1976)						X
Keating v. Holston's Ambulance Service (1989)						X
Fiser v. City of Ann Arbor (1983)						X
Lakoduk v. Cruger (1956)						X
Rutherford v. State (1979)						X
Simkins v. Barcus (1951)						X

Table 3.2
ADMINISTRATIVE RULINGS OF VARIOUS VEHICULAR PURSUIT CASES.

	Government Liability	*Officer Conduct & Force*	*Negligence*	*Due Care*	*Policy & Training*
Tennessee v. Garner (1985)		X			
Graham v. Connor (1989)		X			
Fiser v. City of Ann Arbor (1983)	X				
Canton v. Harris (1989)	X				
Gibson v. Pasadena (1987)	X				
West v. United States (1985)					X
Brooks v. Lundeen (1981)			X		
Oklahoma v. Tuttle (1985)	X				
Monroe v. Pape (1961)	X				
Monell v. Department of Social Services (1978)	X				
Kisbey v. California (1984)	X				
Silva v. City of Albuquerque (1980)				X	
Thornton v. Shore (1983)				X	
Vicknair v. Malbrough (1986)				X	
Lee v. Mitchell Funeral Home Ambulance Service (1980)				X	
Stark v. City of Los Angeles (1985)				X	
Zulauf v. State (1983)					X
Dodge v. Stine (1984)					X
Smith v. City of West Point (1985)					X

against the plaintiff was "not because the challenged force [of the pursuit] occurred in relation to a high-speed chase, but because his allegations of a substantive due process violation are rooted in negligence and allege, at most, a reckless disregard of safety" (*Davis v. Township of Hillsdale,* 1999, p. 4). Here the plaintiff was unable to establish police negligence and reckless disregard for safety despite the fact that the officers in questions acted against written policy.

Helseth v. Burch (2001)

Finally, a case worth mentioning, filed in the Court of Appeals, 8th Circuit, concerns a police pursuit in which a fleeing suspect collided with the defendant, killing the passenger and seriously injuring the plaintiff, leaving him quadriplegic. The plaintiff in this case filed suit against the pursuing officer alleging numerous constitutional violations. The court dismissed all but the plaintiff's substantive due process claim, deciding that Burch, the pursuing officer, denied qualified immunity, "conducted the pursuit with deliberate indifference to public safety" (p. 2). While no formal ruling has been handed down by the Court, this case could have a lasting impact on the processes involved in writing pursuit policy, as officer Burch was not acting against established departmental policy. The Court claimed in the filed petition that the officer was relying solely on existing guidelines while in the course of his pursuit, paying no heed to the safety of the general public.

Legal issues aside, there is a definite need for adequate policy relating to vehicular pursuits. Officers' discretion and performance must be properly guided before they can become efficient and effective law enforcers. Not only is a policy designed as legal protection for the agency, but officer development and the protection of the general public must also be under consideration as administrators outline a pursuit policy. As stated by James Fyfe (1979), there is a need for written departmental policy, "To do otherwise is to simply leave employees 'in the dark' in the expectation that they will intuitively divine the proper and expected course of action in the performance of their duties. . . . Discretion must be reasonably exercised within the parameters of the expectations of the community, the courts, the legislature and the organization itself" (p. 1).

ELEMENTS OF POLICY

As administrators and policymakers strive to identify issues of liability, it is their next responsibility to understand the areas inherent in a more encompassing policy. Departmental orders or directives should become a standard part of every law enforcement organization. Specific departmental orders and directives form the administrative foundation upon which the organization rests. Without a firm foundation, eventually an organization will become a target for liability and negligence suits. The administrative foundation of a department must specify the parameters of organizational behavior through policies, procedures, and rules or regulations. Authority, responsibility, and duties of each rung of the hierarchical ladder are contained in departmental policy (Carter, 1986).

In light of the recent litigation, it is imperative that each police department, no matter how small, have precise, written, comprehensive, and substantively strong policy and directives. Administrators and policymakers must be aware of the differences in terminology of the specific directives contained in the composition of the policy. Policy, objectives, procedures, rules, general orders, special orders, memoranda, and written directives are each unique entities unto themselves and each provide a small portion of the larger departmental directive. Appendix A provides a detailed listing of each of the unique elements required of any sound policy statement.

TRAINING

Once administrators and policymakers are adept at recognizing when an issue might pose a problem of negligence or liability, it is necessary to consider the methods by which the new policy is to be disseminated to officers in the department. Administrators must acknowledge the importance of the use of training, supervision, evaluation, and guidance when presenting officers with policy.

One strategy to understand and appreciate the domain of police pursuits is within the frame of police use of force. In much the same manner that a police firearm is considered an instrument of deadly force, so it is that the patrol cruiser can, at times, be a mechanism of death. As Alpert and Anderson (1986) have stated, ". . . when a police officer engages in a high-speed chase in a high-powered police car, that vehicle becomes a potentially deadly weapon" (p. 2). The myriad of liability and legal issues contained within the sphere of police pursuits are extremely interesting and important to understand for the greater good of society.

The argument can also be established that the constitutional debates developed out of pursuit litigation parallel those generated by instances of police use of force. Many of the same legal tactics and issues involved in use of force cases are utilized in suits alleging liability or negligence in instances of police pursuit. Thus, as the topic of pursuit is of considerable consequence to the field of policing, it is perhaps wise to couch such polemic in the context of the police use of force.

Additionally, it is incumbent upon administrators to place constraints upon officers' use of force. The incorporation of a use of force continuum in policy is one technique to curtail unrestrained uses of force by officers. There are numerous use of force continuums available for a department to utilize in its use of force policy. A department should critically evaluate a use of force continuum, examining the model to determine if it easily understandable and easily recalled by officers under stressful circumstances. It is also necessary for a department to incorporate a statement into the policy dealing with such issues as officer age, size, gender, strength, skill, injury, and exhaustion. A strong affirmative stance by the department will provide officers with confidence and support when trying to make decisions in the field (1992).

Due to the fact that the use of force does not occur in a vacuum, it is imperative that officers be properly trained in use of force techniques as a separate entity. Many departments train officers in defense techniques in a static environment. Recruits never experience a realistic training scenario. Thus, it is vital that training in the use of force be as realistic in nature as possible. This allows officers an opportunity to evaluate their own understanding of the department's policies regarding force. Areas of potential difficulties for officers in the field include handcuffing suspects, transporting prisoners, searching suspects, extracting suspects from vehicles, and making arrests following pursuits (O'Linn, 1992).

Not only is it imperative for line officers to be properly trained, it is also important for supervisory personnel to understand and appreciate the training that such officers receive. Frequently supervisory and administrative personnel fail to continue with updated hands-on training. The result of this neglect by administrators and supervisors is not only a loss of technical expertise, but a loss of understanding concerning this fundamental portion of a field training officer's (FTO's) duty. As stated by O'Linn (1992), "FTO's must possess a thorough understanding of current use-of-force training and policy as it was provided to recent graduates of the police academy, since new officers look to the FTO for guidance on implementing their new skills" (p. 53).

One potential result of the lack of administrators' continued training is a failure to consistently judge instances of the use of force by officers in the field. Without the same training as field officers, administrators and supervisors may not evaluate a situation in the same manner as officers who were trained by departmental instructors. The consequence of differing evaluation schema can be a dichotomy between rules followed by line officers and those adhered to by administrators. This inconsistency leads only to confusion and morale problems. It may also lead to hesitancy by officers in the field, public distrust of the department, and increased liability exposure for the organization and its employees (O'Linn, 1992).

To lessen the risk of liability, a periodic review of use of force incidents may indicate a trend within the organization. Analyzing use of force incidents in terms of various techniques employed, devices used, individual problems, an indication of officers' misunderstanding policy, lack of confidence, or lack of self-control is prudent for administrators seeking ways to lessen potential liability risks for the organization.

Officers also require guidance concerning the proper understanding of the department's use of force policy. Officers are required to be split-second decision-makers and they depend upon the guidance and supervision of the training officers to provide them with the confidence and comprehension to act with deliberation and speed. The law enforcement agency needs to provide its officers with precise and consistent appraisal during training and evaluation.

CONCLUSION

In summation, there are a myriad of legal and constitutional issues surrounding police vehicular pursuits. Due to the inherent dangerousness associated with emergency driving, legal questions have arisen as to what constitutes an emergency situation. During an actual emergency, officers are allowed by law to disobey traffic signals and posted speed limits but are nonetheless obliged to drive with due care for the safety of all other pedestrians and motor vehicles. The courts have been called upon numerous times to decide precisely what constitutes an emergency situation under which officers are allowed to disregard traffic signals and speed limits.

The court has ruled that even if a situation proves not to be an actual emergency, the police are not liable if the responding officer honestly believes the situation to be an emergency. Here, the court found that an "officer must be involved in emergency use of the vehicle and the officer must reasonably feel that an actual emergency exists" (Kappeler, 1993, p. 99). The Washington Supreme Court had already laid out a similar ruling when it stated that, "The test for determining whether a publicly owned vehicle is at a given time responding to an emergency call is not whether an emergency in fact exists at the time but rather whether the vehicle is being used in responding to an emergency call. Whether the vehicle is being so used depends upon the nature of the call that is received and the situation as then perceived to the mind of the driver" (*Lakoduk v. Cruger,* 1956, p. 699).

Municipal liability is also of fundamental importance to police administrators as the actions of individual officers can have a dramatic impact on the agency as a whole. It was in this regard that the Supreme Court would, in time, expose municipalities to unprecedented liability when it ruled that municipalities were not liable as "persons" under Section 1983. The Court later overturned this decision, stating that municipalities were liable as persons under Section 1983. It concluded that, "the legislative history of the act supported a statutory construction that defined "persons" to include municipalities" (Lewis, 1991, p. 556).

The duties required of police officers arise from various sources: law, custom, judicial decisions, and departmental policy. Police officers have a duty to protect the citizenry from unnecessary and unreasonable harm while simultaneously pursuing and apprehending law violators. The legal duty of protection and breach of that duty can place officers and departments alike at risk for claims of liability and negligence. Administrators must caution officers to proceed with due care whenever engaging in pursuit of a violator.

It is evident that the creation of policy with regard to pursuits is a complicated, analytical process. Administrators and policymakers must be aware of current liability trends, tort law, federal civil rights law, negligibility requirements, and liability issues. These legal details must then be incorporated into a concise, available, and comprehensible policy. Officers must be thoroughly trained on the proper use of force and the implications for improper conduct in the field. As administrators develop and implement policy, they lessen any chances of subsequent liability or negligence suits from becoming reality.

REFERENCES

Alpert, G. P., & Anderson, P. (1986). The most deadly force: Police pursuits. *Justice Quarterly, 3:* 1–14.

Bickel v. City of Downey, 238 CalRptr. 351 (Ct.App. 1987).

Brooks v. Lundeen, 364 NE2d 423 (1981).

Brown v. City of New Orleans, 464 So.2d 976 (La. App. 1985).

Brown v. City of Pinellas Park, 557 So.2d 161 (Fla. Dist. Ct.App. 1990).

Brower v. County of Inyo, 817 F.2d 540 (1987).

Canton v. Harris, 109 S.Ct. 1197 (1989).

Carter, D. L. (1986). Police deviance. Cincinnati, OH: Anderson.

Carter, D. L., & Payne, D. M. (1988). *An evaluation of the Delhi Township police department.* Liability of the police officer and the police organization.

City of Akron v. Charley, 440 N.E. 2d 837 (1982).

City of Sacramento v. Sacramento Superior Court in and for Sacramento County, 131 Cal.App. 3d 715 (1982).

Clapp, J. E. (1996). *Random House legal dictionary.* New York: Random House.

Davis v. Township of Hillside, 1999 Misc. 2d 135 (1983).

Del Carmen, R. V. (1986). *Potential liabilities of probation and parole officers.* Cincinnati, OH: Anderson.

Dodge v. Stine, 739 F.2d 1279 (1984).

Fiser v. City of Ann Arbor, 339 N.W. 2d 413 (Mich. 1983).

42 U.S.C. 1983.

Fowler v. North Carolina Department of Crime Control, 376 So.2d 11 (N.C. App. 1989).

Fyfe, J. J. (1979). Administrative interventions on police shooting discretion: An empirical examination. *Journal of Criminal Justice, 7*(4): 309–323.

Georgia Department of Public Safety v. Collins, 140 Ga.App. 884 (1977).

Gibson v. Pasadena, 148 Cal.Rptr. 68 (Cal. App. 2nd Dist. 1987).

Graham v. Connor, 109 S.Ct. 1865 (1989).

Hall, J. C. (1988). Police use of deadly force to arrest: A Constitutional standard. *FBI Law Enforcement Bulletin, 57*(7): 20–29.

Hamilton v. Town of Palo, 244 N.W.2d 329 (Iowa 1976).

Helseth v. Burch, 258 F.3d 867 (2001).

Johnson v. State of California, 447 P.2d 352 (Cal. 1987).

Kappeler, V. E. (1993). *Critical issues in police liability.* Prospect Heights, IL: Waveland Press.

Kappeler, V. E., & del Carmen, R. V. (1988). Police civil liability for failure to arrest drunk drivers. *Police Chief,* October: 102–106.

Keating v. Holston's Ambulance Service Inc., 546 So.2d 911 (La. Ct. App. 1989).

Kisbey v. State of California, 682 P.2d 1093 (1984).

Knaggs v. Lewis, 287 Mich. 431 (1939).

Lakoduk v. Cruger, 296 P.2d 690 (Wash. 1956).

Lee v. Mitchell Funeral Home Ambulance Service, 606 P.2d 259 (1980).

Lewis, K. L. (1991). Section 1983: A matter of policy-current overview of municipal liability. *Michigan Bar Journal,* June: 556–559.

Littell v. Maloney, 3 Kan.App. 2d 240 (1979).

Mason v. Britton, 534 P.2d. 1360 (Wash. 1975).

Michigan Compiled Laws Annotated, 1949, as amended. Section 691.1405.

Monell v. Department of Social Services 436 U.S. 658 1978.

Monroe v. Pape 365 U.S. 167 1961.

Oklahoma v. Tuttle 471 U.S. 808 1985.

O'Linn, M. K. (1992). The gaps in the use-of-force policies and training. *The Police Chief,* February: 52–54.

Payne, D. M., & Corley, C. (1994). Police pursuits: Correlates of the failure to report. *American Journal of Police, 13*(4): 47–72.

Riggs v. State, 488 So.2d 443 (La.App. 1986).

Rutherford v. State, 605 P.2d 16 (1979).

Semple v. Hope, 15 Ohio St. 3d 372 (1984).

Siegel, L. J. (1989). *Criminology* (3rd ed.). St. Paul, MN: West.

Silva v. Albuquerque, 94 N.M. 332 (1980).

Silver, I. (1991). *Police civil liability.* New York: Matthew Bender.

Simkins v. Barcus, 168 Pa.Super. 195 (1951).

Smith v. City of West Point, 475 So. 2d 816 (1985).

Stanulonis v. Marzec, 649 F.Supp. 1536 (1986).

Stark v. City of Los Angeles, 168 Cal.App. 3d 276 (1985).

Swanson, C. R., Territo, L., & Taylor, R. W. (1993). *Police administration* (3rd ed.). New York: Macmillan.

Tennessee v. Garner, 471 U.S. 1 (1985).

Thornont v. Shore, 666 P.2d 655 (Kan. 1983).

Vicknair v. Malbrough, 482 So. 2d 45 (1986).

West v. United States, 617 F.Supp. 1015 (C.D. Cal. 1985).

Zulauf v. State, 119 Misc. 2d 135 (1983).

Chapter 4

STATE TORT LAW

Once a law enforcement administration becomes familiar with the myriad of issues involved in liability and negligence, it is still incumbent upon the organization to underscore their knowledge with an adequate understanding of state tort law as it applies to police liability. Although many instances of police negligence and liability are litigated in federal court, there are many ways a citizen may bring suit against a law enforcement officer or department under state tort law.

Although federal law has many proclamations against police misconduct, state law has its share or precepts discouraging police indiscretion. Under state law, and officer, many be charged with "penal code provisions specifically addressing public officers for offenses such as official oppression or official misconduct" (Carter & Payne, 1988, p. 119). It is also true that an officer could be charged with a standard criminal offense such as assault if the officer in question used improper force against a civilian. It is a safe assumption that if an officer were charged with gross misconduct the department and jurisdiction would also be held liable for a civil lawsuit.

While it is true that the probability of an officer or department being held criminally liable is not dramatically high, the possibility of a civil suit is, indeed, much higher. Many civil lawsuits aimed at police personnel are based on state tort law (Carter & Payne, 1988).

A tort may be defined as, "a wrong, either intentional or unintentional (as when caused by negligence), wherein the action of one person causes injury to the person or property of another in violation of a legal duty imposed by law" (Carter & Payne, 1988, p. 119). The very word "tort" is derived from the Latin "tortus," meaning "bent or twisted" (Kappeler, 1993, p. 17). The first use of the term is thought to have occurred after the Norman conquest of 1066.

TORT v. CRIME

To better understand the conceptualization behind a tort, it is necessary to learn the primary distinction between a tort and a crime. Crimes are offenses against the state that exist in a codified form and are punishable by fines, community service, probation, imprisonment, or death. It is believed in Western law that if an individual is victimized by a criminal act, it is the entire society that is damaged by the violation. As such, the perpetrator of a criminal violation is punished by the state, not by the individual victim (Swanson, Territo, & Taylor, 1993). For an individual perpetrator to be found guilty of a criminal violation, a court of law must find the person guilty beyond a reasonable doubt (Barrineau, 1987).

A tort, however, is "conduct that interferes with the private interests of people or their property" (Kappeler, 1993, p. 18). An individual claiming a violation of a personal interest may bring legal action against the offending party in civil court, rather than invoking criminal proceedings. In a tort action, the injured party is referred to as the plaintiff, much as in a criminal suit, but the defendant is often referred to as the tort feasor (Barrineau, 1987).

A tort, unlike a crime, is rectified by monetary awards and damages. An offending party in a civil suit is not punished by imprisonment or probation as so often occurs in criminal proceedings. Another significant distinction between a tort and a crime is the level of proof required by the court. In a tort action, the plaintiff need only demonstrate that the defendant violated the personal interests of the litigant by a mere preponderance of evidence. Hence, the level of proof is much lower than that required in a criminal court.

Many people become confused when torts and crimes are discussed in conjunction with one another. Much as the O.J. Simpson case illustrated, there are occasions when a tort can also be a crime. Plaintiffs can seek damages in civil court once criminal proceedings have concluded. Cases involving police use of deadly force are often litigated in both criminal as well as civil court. A police officer using deadly force or excessive force can be charged criminally with assault, manslaughter, or even murder. The plaintiff, or relatives or the plaintiff, can then seek civil damages once the prosecutor has completed criminal proceedings. Although this scenario is relatively rare, law enforcement officers can be tried both criminally and civilly for instances of gross misconduct according to tort law.

Tort actions can have devastating results for individual police officers, municipalities, and law enforcement agencies. Plaintiffs in tort suits have three methods of compensation available to them: declaratory relief, injunctive relief, and monetary relief (del Carmen, 1986). In declaratory relief, the court declares that the officer and/or department acted improperly and bears liability for the actions leading to the injury or damage (del Carmen, 1986). In injunctive relief, the court grants the plaintiff's request for a change in operations or policy. The importance and impact of this type of relief cannot be underscored. Court mandates to alter operations or policy can be costly. The organization has little option but to adhere to the guidelines established by the court and proceed with the changes as ordered. Finally, monetary relief can be quite costly for officers and departments. Under monetary relief, the defendant, or tort feasor, is required to pay the plaintiff for damages suffered. Actual monetary relief can be damages for medical expenses, property damage, or lost wages. Punitive damages can then also be awarded a plaintiff in a tort action. Punitive damages refer to the pain and suffering of the plaintiff. There is no limit to the amount of damages awarded in monetary relief. The amount can climb into the millions of dollars. This can have disastrous consequences for an organization or municipality if the damages awarded exceed the jurisdiction's liability insurance coverage. There have been instances where municipalities have been required to sell property and even issue bonds to raise the funds required of the courts in monetary damages.

LIABILITY

There are jurisdictions across the country where police negligence is barred by statutes immunizing officers from liability claims in the emergency operation of vehicles (Kappeler, 1993). Generally, these statutes immunize officers from claims of liability when they attempt to apprehend escaping suspects. An example of such a statute was interpreted by the California Supreme Court in the ruling that, "the

purpose of the legislation was to immunize public entities and employees from the entire spectrum of potential injuries caused by persons
actually or about to be deprived of their freedom who take physical
measures of one kind or another to avoid the constraint or escape from
it" (*Kisbey v. State of California,* 1984, p. 1096).

If a tort lawsuit is to be brought against an officer or department, it
is necessary first that the officer or department act with care toward the
suing party. If the duty of the officer was breached and that subsequent
breach created the proximate cause of injury to the party as a result,
liability may be established. "Injury" in such a case is not limited
merely to physical harm, but includes injury to the rights of the person under consideration. There are a myriad of torts for which an officer can be found liable: wrongful death, use of excessive force, invasion of privacy, libel or slander, negligent vehicle operation, or negligent administration of first aid (Siegel, 1989).

NEGLIGENCE TORT

In the United States, as in most developed, industrialized nations of
the world, government officials are called upon to conduct their daily
operations within the scope of what is reasonable behavior to most
people. Society imposes a legal duty upon government employees to
behave in a manner that does not place the citizenry in unreasonable
risk of harm. This duty is never so evident as in the case of law
enforcement officials.

When police officers or law enforcement officials conduct their
daily operations in such a manner as to jeopardize the safety and well
being of the general populace, the individual responsible for such
gross misconduct will be held accountable. Much of what is considered unreasonable or risky behavior in the realm of law enforcement
is litigated under negligence tort.

Negligence is defined as "inadvertent behavior that results in damage or injury" (Kappeler, 1993, p. 23). In negligence litigation, defendants are not held liable unless they foresaw, or should have antici-
pated, the damaging results of their actions. The key factor in negligence suits is "reasonableness" (Swanson, Territo, & Taylor, 1993). An
attorney involved in a negligence suit would ask whether the action or
conduct would seem reasonable in the eyes of the court. If the court

finds the conduct of the officer reasonable under the specific circumstances, then liability does not hold for the actions under consideration. Negligence tort differs from intentional tort, which will be discussed later, in that a lesser degree of forseeability is required in negligence tort to substantiate a claim of negligence.

Many instances of negligence have arisen in the courts dealing with police vehicular chases in which officers violate common traffic regulations, such as running stop signs or speeding (*Brown v. City of New Orleans,* 1985; *Riggs v. State,* 1986; *Brown v. City of Pinellas Park,* 1990). In cases involving excessive speed the single factor of high speed, is not considered conclusive evidence of police negligence (*Brown v. City of New Orleans,* 1986; *Riggs v. State,* 1986). In cases involving a police pursuit, the courts will generally consider a wide variety of factors in determining negligence. Factors such as justification of the pursuit, actual vehicle operation, circumstances of operation, and external factors such as weather and road conditions are each considered by the courts in determining police negligence.

In instances where a pursuing officer has violated traffic regulations such as running stop signs or disregarding traffic signals, the courts will consider the extent to which the officer operated the police vehicle with blatant disregard for the safety and well-being of the general public. When taking into account excessive speeds or other external factors during a police high-speed chase, courts have isolated specific actions occurring during a pursuit and separated them from behaviors constituting conclusive evidence of officer negligence (Kappeler, 1993). The courts have found that officers operating an emergency vehicle in excess of the posted speed limit does not constitute negligence in and of itself (*Brown v. City of New Orleans,* 1986; *Riggs v. State,* 1986). The distinctions found in *Brown v. City of New Orleans* (1986), *Riggs v. State* (1986), and *Brown v. City of Pinellas Park* (1990) are based on the totality of circumstances approach to reasonableness the courts have so often utilized.

The courts distinguish between the actual operation of the police vehicle and the original decision of the officer to pursue the suspect. Using this standard, the courts have held that the reasonableness standard is triggered only by the operation of the vehicle and not the original decision to pursue (Kappeler, 1993). The original decision of the officer to pursue a suspect cannot, in itself, substantiate a claim of negligence. Kappeler (1993) has listed each item or element courts have used in consideration of a determination of negligence. Each element can be grouped into four classifications, or zones of negligence: justification of pursuit, actual vehicle operation, circumstances of operation, and external factors.

Justification factors considered by the courts include whether:

1. a real or apparent emergency existed (*Hamilton v. Town of Palo*, 1976; *Keating v. Holston's Ambulance Service, Inc.*, 1989)
2. the offender's conduct was serious (*Gibson v. Pasadena*, 1978)
3. alternatives to pursuit were available to the officer (*Mason v. Britton*, 1978)
4. apprehension of the suspect was feasible

Factors in the actual physical operation of the vehicle considered by the courts include:

1. speed at which the vehicle is operated
2. use of emergency equipment (*Fowler v. North Carolina Department of Crime Control*, 1989)
3. violation of traffic regulations
4. disregard of traffic control devices (*Brown v. City of Pinellas Park*, 1990)

Factors in the circumstances of operation considered by the courts include:

1. physical conditions of the roadway
2. weather conditions (*Bickel v. City of Downey*, 1987)
3. density of traffic (*Brown v. City of Pinellas Park*, 1990)
4. presence of pedestrians
5. presence of audio or visual warning devises
6. area of pursuit (*Brown v. City of Pinellas Park*, 1990)

External factors considered by the courts include:

1. violation of departmental policy regarding police pursuits
2. officer's training in pursuit driving (*West v. United States*, 1985)
3. physical and visual condition of the police vehicle

Despite the courts acceptance of the totality of circumstances approach to dealing with police pursuits, determining negligence has become a highly complicated endeavor. In court, a defendant must demonstrate four basic elements to substantiate a claim of negligence: a legal duty, a breach of that duty, proximate cause, and actual damage or injury. The absence of any single factor can eliminate the court's finding of negligence.

LEGAL DUTY

The legal duty of a police officer is quite specific. A legal duty is behavior or conduct recognized by the courts which requires police officers to take action or, in other circumstances, to refrain from taking action (Kappeler, 1993). These duties can arise from laws, customs, judicial decisions, or departmental policy.

Most negligence suits in the past were unsuccessful in establishing legal duty of an officer. Individuals claiming that an officer owed them a specific legal duty were unsuccessful in convincing the courts that they were owed that duty. Courts ruled that police officers owed a legal duty of protection to the general public, but not to any one specific individual (Kappeler, 1993).

In more recent rulings, this has changed slightly. Courts now recognize that under certain circumstances the police may, indeed, owe a special legal duty to individuals. This is especially true in cases where the actions of the police might set an individual apart from other members of society (Kappeler, 1993). For example, if an officer stopped a driver under the influence of narcotics but failed to make an arrest, subsequent courts might find that a special relationship had been created between the patrol officer and the motoring public (Kappeler, 1993). If such a case were to be brought before a court, the officer could be found liable for any damage the intoxicated driver might inflict (Kappeler & del Carmen, 1988).

BREACH OF DUTY

Findings of legal duty are not, in themselves, sufficient to establish police liability. As stated previously, a plaintiff must also demonstrate that an officer breached a legal duty owed to the individual. A breach of duty is established from a determination of factual situations. To establish breach of duty in a court, the plaintiff must demonstrate that a special circumstance existed that sets them apart from the general public. As in the earlier example of the intoxicated driver, a plaintiff might be successful in establishing a special relationship existing between the officer and the intoxicated driver. The failure of the officer to arrest the driver could be considered a breach of duty if the driver caused some subsequent accident or injury.

As in police pursuits, drivers of emergency vehicles have a duty to the public to drive with due care for the safety of people using the roadway. For an officer to drive carelessly or recklessly, that could be considered in court a breach of the legal duty owed the general public to drive with due care for safety.

PROXIMATE CAUSE

If a plaintiff is successful in establishing legal duty and breach of duty in court, he/she must still demonstrate the concept of proximate cause. Proximate cause is determined by asking the question, but for the officer's conduct, would the plaintiff have sustained the injury or damage (Kappeler, 1993). This question is designed to prevent a plaintiff from trying to establish police liability in instances where the damage or injury would have been sustained despite the behavior of the officer. If the answer to this question is "no" then the plaintiff has established proximate cause. If a plaintiff can establish proximate cause, then it follows that the officer can be held liable for the damage in question.

As discussed in greater depth in Chapter 3, police pursuits are replete with instances where courts must determine if the officer was the proximate cause of an accident or injury. Despite proper training and driving with due care, officers will, nonetheless, be involved in the occasional accident. It has been a rule within the courts that if an officer has not acted in a negligent or unreasonable manner and cannot be properly shown to be the precise cause of the injury or damage sustained, then liability is not established.

DAMAGE OR INJURY

Once a plaintiff has successfully established legal duty, breach of duty, and proximate cause in a court of law, it is still incumbent upon them to demonstrate the existence of a damage or injury. A civil suit will fail unless the plaintiff can firmly establish that they have sustained some tangible injury or damage due to the actions of the officer. In addition, the plaintiff must demonstrate that their injury or damage significantly interfered with an interest or property. The damage or injury must also exist within the "here and now." The possibility of future damages or injuries are not sufficient to establish officer liability in civil court.

INTENTIONAL TORT

An intentional tort is precisely as it infers. The officer's behavior or conduct was voluntary and, perhaps, intentional. Intentional tort differs significantly from negligence tort due to the fact that the behavior or conduct involved in litigation does not have to be proven to be negligent. It simply has to have occurred. However, as an important cautionary statement, it must be remembered that the term "intentional" does not mean the officer inflicted the damage or injury deliberately, simply that the decision to engage in the behavior or conduct that led to the damage or injury was intentional. Intentional torts generally involve such police actions as assault, false arrest, false imprisonment, or malicious prosecution.

Intentional torts are those behaviors that can be substantially certain to cause injury or damage. For example, an officer who shoots an unarmed suspect during a police foot pursuit might accidentally kill the suspect when the intention was to simply bring the suspect to a halt. In court, for the purposes of an intentional tort, the plaintiff must only demonstrate that the officer intended to discharge the pistol. For the purposes of liability, it makes no difference whether the officer intended to kill, wound, or stop the suspect. The intention of the officer to stop the suspect, not to kill, is irrelevant. Assuming the officer intended to discharge the firearm and could be reasonable certain of inflicting damage or injury, liability could be found by the court.

There have been many instances in which intentional tort has been used by plaintiffs in wrongful death claims against the police. Police officers who either take the life of a citizen or fail to prevent the death of a citizen can be held liable for wrongful death. Police vehicular pursuits can be a source for wrongful death claims. Claims of wrongful death arise in instances of police use of deadly force. Firearms and squad cars are the most frequent sources of deadly force utilized by police.

Wrongful death laws are intended to compensate families of individuals killed by inappropriate police conduct. In addition to awards for the family of the deceased, punitive damages can also be awarded. Individual police officers, as well as the department, can be a source for monetary award in instances of wrongful death.

STRICT LIABILITY TORT

As stated by Kappeler (1993), "Strict liability torts are normally associated with behaviors that are so dangerous or hazardous that a person who engages in such behavior can be substantially certain the conduct will result in injury or damage" (p. 19). Actions of this type are socially and legally deemed inappropriate. Thus, individuals engaging in such conduct are held liable for any damages or injuries that result. Under strict liability tort, the officer's mental state is not a consideration; it is simply a question of whether the officer engaged in the behavior in question.

When a strict liability case goes before the court, it is up to the court to decide if the officer or department should bear the financial costs associated with the damage or injury inflicted (Kappeler, 1993). There are few instances where police officers face any real concern over strict liability tort. However, courts have found police policy in instances in which officers are trained to use military style tactics to halt drug trafficking to be capable of placing officer at risk for strict liability risks (Kappeler, 1993). There have been those individuals advocating the use of war planes by the police to curb drug trafficking. A policy

Table 4.1
DIFFERENCES BETWEEN LEVELS OF STATE TORTS.

Type of Tort	Behaviors	Elements
Strict Liability	Extremely dangerous	Conduct & damage or injury
Intentional	Purposive behaviors likely to result in damage	Knowledge, foreseeability & damage or injury
Negligence	Inadvertent & unreasonable behaviors	Legal duty, breach, proximate cause & damage or injury

approving a tactic such as this could place officers at risk for a claim of strict liability.

Kappeler (1993) has devised an easy method by which to differentiate between torts and crimes. Table 4.1 demonstrates the differences between the three types of torts explained. The type of tort is listed alongside the various behaviors leading up to the tort action and the many elements included in each tort.

EMERGENCY OPERATION v. NONEMERGENCY DRIVING

The operation of vehicles by the police can be classified into two distinct categories: routine and emergency operations. Police officers are required to operate vehicles during the performance of their daily duties. An officer operating a vehicle under normal, routine conditions is held to the same standard of reasonableness required of the general public. Under routine conditions, any accident or injury incurred during the performance of patrol duties is litigated under the general theory of negligence (Kappeler, 1993). If a violation of law is to be considered negligent, the complainant must demonstrate that the law was designed to prevent the damage or injury inflicted. In addition, the law must have been designed to protect a specific class of persons (Kappeler, 1993).

The second type of operation of vehicles by police officers involves emergency situations. Due to the inherent dangers posed by the use of emergency vehicles in responses by police, all states have enacted statutes governing the operation of emergency vehicles (Silver, 1991). Many jurisdictions grant emergency vehicles limited statutory immunity for any violations of state or municipal traffic regulation incurred during an emergency response (Kappeler, 1993). Thus, police officers are afforded some level of protection while responding to emergency calls for assistance.

Questions have arisen as to what constitutes an emergency situation for police officers. This query is to be determined by the courts based on situational factors and individual officers' perception (Kappeler, 1993). It has been decided by the courts that, basically, an "officer must be involved in emergency use of the vehicle and the officer must reasonably feel that an actual emergency exists" (Kappeler, 1993, p. 99). Previously, the Washington Supreme Court had ruled that, "The test for determining whether a publicly owned vehicle is at a given time responding to an emergency call is not whether an emergency in fact exists at the time but rather whether the vehicle is being used in responding to an emergency call. Whether the vehicle is being so used depends upon the nature of the call that is received and the situation as then perceived to the mind of the driver" (*Lakoduk v. Cruger,* 1956, p. 699).

In some instances, for purposes of immunity, courts hold that the chase or attempted apprehension of a law violator is not always an emergency. Therefore, an officer's negligence in violating traffic regulations is determined by the surrounding circumstances dictating the use of the vehicle and the seriousness of the suspect's behavior (*Fiser v. City of Ann Arbor,* 1983). The Michigan Supreme Court stated that "in order for [statutory immunity] to apply, defendants must show that the officers reasonably believed an emergency existed. The chase or apprehension of violators of the law does not necessarily constitute an emergency situation" (*Fiser v. City of Ann Arbor,* 1983, p. 417).

In states with limited statutory immunity, the officer is not held liable for the violation of a state or municipal traffic regulation while responding to an emergency. A violation of a traffic regulation resulting in injury or damage is not conclusive proof of the officer's negligence (Kappeler, 1993). If a plaintiff should desire to establish proof of negligent operation of an emergency vehicle, factors beyond the mere violation of a traffic must be established if the claim of negligence is to be supported. Limited statutory immunity varies from state to state and is restricted to the use of vehicles in actual emergency situations.

CONCLUSION

As can be readily surmised by the summary of state tort law, police officers and administrators face a complex mesh of state tort laws regarding liability and negligence in their daily operations. While it is necessary for administrators and policymakers to understand the many complexities of state tort law in order to decrease or eliminate departmental liability, it is, nonetheless, a duty for patrol officers to appreciate the larger realm of tort law so they might perform their daily patrol duties to better serve the public and protect themselves from liability and negligence concerns. There have been instances of civil litigation nearly bankrupting officers and municipalities. Liability and negligence suits are avoidable if officers and administrators learn to understand and appreciate state tort law.

REFERENCES

Barrineau, H. E. (1987). *Civil liability in criminal justice.* Cincinnati, OH: Anderson.

Bickel v. City of Downey, 238 CalRptr. 351 (Ct.App. 1987).

Brown v. City of New Orleans, 464 So.2d 976 (La. App. 1985).

Brown v. City of Pinellas Park, 557 So.2d 161 (Fla. Dist. Ct.App. 1990).

Carter, D. L., & Payne, D. M. (1988). *An evaluation of the Delhi Township police department.* Liability of the police officer and the police organization.

Del Carmen, R. V. (1986). *Potential liabilities of probation and parole officers.* Cincinnati, OH: Anderson.

Fiser v. City of Ann Arbor, 339 N.W. 2d 413 (Mich. 1983).

Fowler v. North Carolina Department of Crime Control, 376 So.2d 11 (N.C. App. 1989).

Gibson v. Pasadena, 148 Cal.Rptr. 68 (Cal. App. 2nd Dist. 1987).

Hamilton v. Town of Palo, 244 N.W.2d 329 (Iowa 1976).

Kappeler, V. E. (1993). *Critical issues in police liability.* Prospect Heights, IL: Waveland Press.

Kappeler, V. E., & del Carmen, R. V. (1988). Police civil liability for failure to arrest drunk drivers. *Police Chief,* October: 102–106.

Keating v. Holston's Ambulance Service Inc., 546 So.2d 911 (La. Ct. App. 1989).

Kisbey v. State of California, 682 P.2d 1093 (1984).

Lakoduk v. Cruger, 296 P.2d 690 (Wash. 1956).

Mason v. Britton, 534 P.2d. 1360 (Wash. 1975).

Riggs v. State, 488 So.2d 443 (La.App. 1986).

Siegel, L. J. (1989). *Criminology* (3rd ed.). St. Paul, MN: West.

Silver, I. (1991). *Police civil liability.* New York: Matthew Bender.

Swanson, C. R., Territo, L., & Taylor, R. W. (1993). *Police administration* (3rd ed.). New York: Macmillan.

West v. United States, 617 F.Supp. 1015 (C.D. Cal. 1985).

Chapter 5

FEDERAL LIABILITY LAW

The field of police vehicular pursuits is replete with complex, often conflicting legal issues. The consequences of negligence can have far reaching implications for law enforcement agencies as well as individual officers. Litigation can be financially devastating for a department. Administrators and policymakers need to continually update policy so as to effect any revisions necessary to take into consideration recent court rulings. While this is not an appropriate venue for an exhaustive legal analysis of pursuit ramifications, the synopsis below will provide the discriminating reader with a guide to understanding the many legal intricacies involved in police pursuits.

42 U.S.C. § 1983

By far, the single most common method of litigation in the federal court system with respect to police misconduct or abuse of authority begins with 42 U.S.C. § 1983. The reference to this often used law is derived from the fact that suits are brought against a law enforcement organization under the provisions of Section 1983 of Title 42 of the United States Code (Kappeler, 2001). This is euphemistically referred to as a "1983 action." The current trend existing in law enforcement litigation is the vast increase in the number of § 1983 suits being processed through the court system.

Section § 1983 began as a method by which to curb the activities of the Ku Klux Klan in the post-Civil War era. This law, commonly referred to as the Civil Rights Act of 1871, was an attempt to secure the civil and constitutional rights of emancipated slaves (del Carmen,

1991). Section § 1983 was designed to prohibit the deprivation of life, liberty, or property without due process of law. Title 42 of the U.S. Code reads, "Every person who, under color of any statute, ordinance, regulation, custom, or usage, of any State or Territory or he District of Columbia, subjects, or causes to be subjected, any citizen of the United States or other persons within the jurisdiction thereof to the deprivation of any rights, privileges, or immunities secured by the Constitution and laws, shall be liable to the party injured in an action at law, suit in equity, or other proper proceeding for redress. For the purposes of this section, any Act of Congress applicable exclusively to the District of Columbia shall be considered to be a statute of the District of Columbia" (p. 1).

After 90 years of seeming obscurity, Section § 1983 was brought back to life by the U.S. Supreme Court in the case of *Monroe v. Pape* (365 U.S. 167 1961). This case centered upon an incident in which a plaintiff sued 13 Chicago police officers, claiming the officers stormed into his place of residence without a warrant, forced family members out of bed at gunpoint, subjected them to physical and verbal assault, and ransacked the house. The decision of the Court stated that in instances in which a police officer is alleged to have acted improperly, that officer can be sued in federal court by an allegation that the plaintiff was deprived of the Constitutional right to be free from unreasonable searches and seizure as mandated under the Fourth Amendment (*Monroe v. Pape,* 1961). In this case, the officers named in the suit were alleged to have searched the plaintiff's home without a search warrant.

This case was also noteworthy due to the fact that the Court found that because Section § 1983 provided for a civil action, the plaintiff need not prove that the defendants acted with "specific intent to deprive a person of a federal right" (p. 187). In addition, the Court concluded that municipalities, here the City of Chicago, were immune from liability under the statute. The Court ruled that municipalities were not liable as "persons" under Section § 1983 (Hall, 1988).

Critical to understanding the proper use of Section § 1983 in federal litigation is the fact that an alleged violation must have occurred while the offending officer was acting "under color of State law." Stated differently, the officer must be on duty and acting within the scope of employment as a sworn law enforcement official (Swanson, Territo, & Taylor, 1993). As stated by the Court, "Misuse of power, possessed by virtue of state law and made possible only because the wrongdoer is clothed with the authority of state law, is action taken under color of state law" (*United States v. Classic,* 1941, p. 326).

The courts have been forced to view police pursuits in a use of force context. A use of force issue is traditionally litigated under 42 U.S.C. § 1983. In *Baker v. McCollan* (1979) the Court decided that the initial inquiry into any § 1983 suit must isolate and identify the constitutional violation before any subsequent action can begin. As stated previously, most pursuit cases will involve some issues relevant to the Fourth Amendment's prohibition against unreasonable searches and seizures. It is necessary to isolate those violations prior to any court actions.

Under Section 1983, it is necessary to establish officer or departmental liability through the presence of four elements: (1) the defendant must be a natural person or a local government; (2) the defendant must be acting under color of law; (3) the violation must be of a constitutional or federally protected right; (4) the violation must reach a constitutional level (Carter & Payne, 1988). For an officer or a department to act under color of law, the entity must be acting "with the appearance of legal authority; in actual or purported performance of one's duties as a state official" (Clapp, 1996, p. 274).

Once liability has been established, the plaintiff in a Section 1983 suit may request three types of relief: monetary relief, declaratory relief, or injunctive relief. Monetary relief, of which there is no set limit, is awarded when defendants are required to pay the plaintiff for damages incurred as a result of actions of the officer. Declaratory relief is characterized by a declaration of the court that the officer and/of department acted improperly and bears the full brunt of responsibility for the actions in question. The court grants, in injunctive relief, the plaintiff's request for a change in operations or behavior of the officer and/or department. The impact of injunctive relief cannot be underestimated. The court can mandate policy and managerial operations for which a department has little choice but to follow.

FOURTEENTH AMENDMENT

Questions have also arisen in regards to various Fourteenth Amendment considerations raised by police pursuits. In *County of Sacramento v. Lewis* (1998), the issue of police culpability was again examined. The case involved the death of a motorcyclist involved in a high-speed police chase. The Court was called upon to determine whether the officers involved in the pursuit had violated the defendant's Fourteenth Amendment guarantee of substantive due process. Litigants claimed that the due process clause had been violated after the officers caused the death of the cyclist through deliberate and reckless indifference to life in a high-speed pursuit. In response to the claim, Justice Souter delivered the Court's decision by stating, "We answer no, and hold that in such circumstances only a purpose to cause harm unrelated to the legitimate object of arrest will satisfy the element of arbitrary conduct shocking to the conscience, necessary for a due process violation" (p. 15).

GOOD FAITH

Plaintiffs opting for litigation under Section § 1983 can pursue damages against government and state officials claiming that the infractions occurred as the officials were acting in their individual capacities rather than official positions (Swanson, Territo, & Taylor, 1993). However, plaintiffs will be required to overcome the good faith, qualified immunity enjoyed by government and state officials. The qualified, good faith immunity did not originate in Section § 1983; it was a product of traditional common law.

The doctrine of good faith immunity states that a public official should not be held liable for discretionary actions occurring in the course of official duties undertaken in good faith (Roberg, Kuykendall, & Novak, 2002). This is especially true with regard to many of the discretionary duties performed by police officers in the performance of their daily operations. It has been argued by the courts that to impose liability upon public officials in instances where official duties were undertaken in good faith would deter their willingness to "execute . . . [their] office with the decisiveness and judgment required by the public good" (*Scheuer v. Rhodes*, 1974, p. 240). Imposing such liability risks in cases where actions were undertaken by a public official in good faith would, in turn, harm the public as such officials would be less willing to place themselves at any risks of liability. To counter such a possibility, Kappeler (2001) has stated that, "if a court determined that the law was not clearly established or that the officer's conduct was reasonable, the officer is to be afforded immunity from liability" (p. 62).

As can be surmised, the courts have struggled to develop an objective test indicating actions undertaken by a public official in "good faith." It would be the case of *Wood v. Strickland* (1975) in which the courts would develop a two-prong test for good faith. Here, the Court stated that the test for good faith should take into account both the subjective state of mind of the public official in question as well as the objective element contained in the alleged violation. The objective element would, by necessity, be a violation of a clearly established legal right.

It would be seven years later, in the case of *Harlow v. Fitzgerald* (1982), that the Court would revise the subjective element of the good faith test, leaving what is currently referred to as the standard of "objective reasonableness." At the time the objective reasonableness standard was finalized, the courts needed only to determine if the legally protected right was clearly established at the time the violation occurred. If the plaintiff cannot demonstrate that a violation of a clearly established law occurred, public officials need only utilize the good faith immunity protection to obtain dismissal of the allegations against them. This immunity available to public officials is designed to protect individuals against liability as they perform daily duties associated with their particular office. Factors utilized by the courts in an effort to determine issues involved in good faith include: (1) the officer acted in accordance with agency rules and regulations, (2) the officers acted pursuant to a statute that is reasonably believed to be valid but is later declared unconstitutional, (3) the officer acted in accordance with orders from a superior that are reasonably believed to be valid, (4) the officer acted in accordance with advice from a legal counsel that is reasonably believed to be valid (del Carmen, 1991, p. 55).

This immunity doctrine is also intended to protect police officers in instances of searches, seizures, and arrests. If an officer can demonstrate that probable cause existed or that an individual had committed a crime, then a search is justified and litigation in federal court is barred (Kappeler, 2001; *Hunter v. Bryant,* 1991). If, after the fact, it can be demonstrated that probable cause did not exist, but the officer was acting on good faith, the officer in question is not held liable. As stated by del Carmen (1991), "Probable cause is so strong a defense in arrest and search and seizure cases that some courts have held that if probable cause is present, the officer is not liable even if malice is involved in the officer's act" (p. 57).

ABSOLUTE IMMUNITY

Under the old system of English common law, police officers were held personally responsible for any damages inflicted if their actions extended beyond the scope of permissible behavior as outlined by their department. This common law rule applied even if an officer was unaware of the precise boundary establish by the department (Swanson, Territo, & Taylor, 1993). As stated by Swanson, Territo, and Taylor (1993), "the rule established one of the traditional risks of policing" (p. 402).

As established by common law, an individual officer was held personally responsible if his/her behavior exceeded the boundaries established by his/her department. An added query centered on the question of whether a supervisor or administrator could be held personally liable for the actions of subordinates as they carried out their daily patrol duties. This quandary was primarily based upon the common law principle of respondent superior. This doctrine is now referred to as vicarious liability in most jurisdictions (Prosser, 1971).

The conceptualization of vicarious liability developed in conjunction with the industrialization of society. It was intended to reflect an effort to allocate liability risks to those individuals and offices who could better assume the financial burden associated with police negligence or liability (Prosser, 1971). Individual officers could rarely afford any claims of liability dispensed by the courts. However, police supervisors and administrators were in a much better position to assume the costs of financial damages so often handed down by the American court system in liability litigation. Despite the intention of the vicarious liability doctrine, American courts remain reluctant to extend the liability risks to police supervisors and administrators (Schmidt, 1976).

The reluctance of courts to extend liability risks onto police supervisors and administrators is based primarily on two rationales. The first rationale for the hesitation of courts to extend the doctrine of vicarious liability is the fact that police administrators and supervisors have limited discretion in hiring decisions (*Parish v. Meyers,* 1924). According to the ruling in *Parish v. Meyers,* "The courts have very generally drawn a distinction between a sheriff and a chief of police, holding that the deputies of the former are selected and appointed by the sheriff and act purely as his representatives, but that police officers are generally not selected exclusively by the chief of police, and are themselves officers and do not act for the chief of police in the performance of the official duties" (p. 633). Therefore, if police administrators and supervisors are not in a position to have the ultimate hiring decision, they should not be held responsible for those individuals they might otherwise have not hired.

The second reason for the hesitation of the court system to extend vicarious liability centers upon the fact that police officers are public officials whose duties are established by government authority (*Jordan v. Kelly*, 1963). Their positions as agents of law enforcement were not created by their immediate supervisor or administrator. They were created by the government. The courts maintain that police administrators and supervisors are not in the capacity to control the actions of their subordinates in the same fashion as their counterparts in private industry (Swanson, Territo, & Taylor, 1993).

Although the courts have been hesitant to extend the doctrine of vicarious liability to police supervisors and administrators, they do not insulate them from liability for the behavior of their subordinates in all instances. If a supervisor or administrator authorizes the tortious actions of a subordinate, was present at the time the infraction occurred, did nothing to halt the misconduct, or collaborated in the activity, partial liability can be extended to that supervisor or administrator (Swanson, Territo, & Taylor, 1993).

The hesitance to extend the doctrine of vicarious liability to supervisors and administrators has been diminished somewhat in recent years. Kenneth Culp Davis, a legal commentator, has reported that the court system as a whole "had abolished chunks of sovereign immunity" by 1978 (Swanson, Territo, & Taylor, 1993). By 1978, only two states still completely adhered to the common law approach that government entities, including police supervisors and administrators, were fully immune from legal challenge (Swanson, Territo, and Taylor, 1993). As stated by Swanson, Territo, & Taylor (1993), "In most states in which abrogation of sovereign immunity has occurred, the abrogation has not been total. In some states, the abrogation is an unconditional waiver of sovereign immunity, but the waiver extends only to certain activities, to cases in which the employee had a particular state of mind, to liability not to exceed a designated monetary amount, or to only a particular level of government" (p. 455). While some states differ as to their approach to the treatment of sovereign immunity, it is clear that the traditional common law approach to the issue has undergone change in the contemporary court system.

While a plaintiff may still sue a governmental entity, a case reaching the federal court system is considered somewhat differently. It is the responsibility of the courts to examine a plaintiff's claim against the government entity in an effort to determine if the requested relief can be imposed upon the entity. The success of the plaintiff's cause depends upon which immunities are available to the defendant, in this case a government entity (Swanson, Territo, & Taylor, 1993). As the court proceeds, those immunities available will be applied to determine whether the defendants remain in the suit and what damages, if any, would be considered appropriate.

In federal litigation against state officials sued as part of their officials capacities, the courts have determined that the Eleventh Amendment precludes monetary rewards and damages (*Hans v. Louisiana*, 1890; *Edelman v. Jordan*, 1974). As iterated by Swanson, Territo, and Taylor (1993), the courts have decided "that the essence of the Eleventh Amendment is its protection of state treasuries against damage awards in federal court (p. 406).

The Eleventh Amendment states, "The judicial power of the United States shall not be construed to extend to any suit in law or equity, commenced or prosecutes against one of the United States by citizens or another state, or by citizens or subjects of any foreign state". While this amendment protects the state treasuries from monetary relief in federal court, it does not preclude the courts from ordering state officials to remedy certain behaviors or policies in the future even if such action requires extensive monetary expenditure from the state treasury (*Alabama v. Pugh*, 1978).

As the Eleventh Amendment and the qualified immunity doctrine were utilized as protection for state officials against liability, the question of immunity in local government was eventually raised. Initially, the Court had determined that legislators had not designed 42 U.S.C. § 1983 to apply to municipal governments (*Monroe v. Pape*, 1961). Thus, municipal government officials were protected by absolute or unqualified immunity by this ruling.

This issue would again come to the Court in the case of *Monell v.*

Department of Social Services (1978). Here, the Court was called upon to reexamine the issue of liability and immunity protecting municipal governments and their officials. The Court would ultimately decide that Section § 1983 had, indeed, been intended to apply to municipal governments and their officials. In addition, the Court concluded that a municipality could not be held liable under Section § 1983 simply because an individual responsible for such a violation was employed by that municipality. The Court maintained that a municipality would be held liable for violations occurring due to a function of an existing policy or procedure. One caveat concerning the Monell verdict centered upon the fact that the Court failed, deliberately or not, to articulate the limits of municipal liability under Section § 1983. As a result, Section § 1983 litigation soared after the Monell ruling.

Due to rising litigation against police agencies after Monell, the Courts were repeatedly called upon to define the limits of municipal liability. It was necessary for the Court to determine when a violation of a federally protected right was due to the enforcement of an existing policy or procedure. It was also necessary to establish precisely when official action could be considered as establishing the policy or procedure responsible for the violation. In *Oklahoma v. Tuttle* (1985), the court determined that a single act of police misconduct could demonstrate that a municipal government policy or procedure was involved in the alleged violation.

COLOR OF LAW

The term "color of law" is translated into an individual who acts in the capacity as a "state actor" and derives power from the state (Roberg, Kuykendall, & Novak, 2002). Therefore, if an officer is performing typical law enforcement duties required of his/her employment, he/she is acting under color of law (Kappeler, 2001). Courts will often define color of law by asking two pertinent questions: (1) Was police power used? or, (2) Did the department authorize the act? (Worrall, 1998).

Questions have arisen as to the conditions under which an officer might not be acting under color of law. Many police departments allow officers to seek employment as private security guards. Pertinent questions have arisen as to when an individual officer may not act under color of law and whether the police organization is held liable for any misconduct under Section § 1983.

Vaughn and Coomes (1995) have provided answers to these questions and noted some important caveats to this segment of Section § 1983 liability. In a review of contemporary case law, they concluded that officers act "under color of law if they invoke police power; if they discharge duties routinely associated with police work, or if they use their authority to lure potential plaintiffs into compromising positions" (p. 398). Therefore, behaviors typically associated with police officers, such as wearing a uniform, making arrests, filing reports, or pursuing suspected law violators indicate that these individuals are acting under color of law.

Whether an officer is acting under color of law is determined from the perspective of the plaintiff (Roberg, Kuykendall, & Novak, 2002). It is necessary to determine if the plaintiff believed the officer was acting under color of law to adequately determine if such intentions were actually occurring. The question of whether an officer is acting under color of law can be summed up in the following indicators as seen in Table 5.1 (Vaughn & Coomes, 1995).

Policymakers must also understand that liability can be both a direct as well as vicarious phenomenon. If an individual is the direct cause of the resultant injury or violation, it is defined by a claim of direct liability. Substituted responsibility, where supervisors, administrators, and others in the hierarchical chain of command are held responsible for the actions of their subordinates, is characteristic of vicarious liability. A plaintiff wishing to establish vicarious liability must demonstrate that the police department acted negligently, or with deliberate indifference, in permitting improper police conduct. Generally, it is necessary for the plaintiff to be required to demonstrate a pattern of misconduct to exist with a department. However, in instances of gross impropriety, it may not be necessary to establish a pattern of behavior.

NEGLIGENT SUPERVISION AND NEGLIGENT TRAINING

According to Swanson, Territo, and Taylor (1993), two of the greatest sources for litigation under Section § 1983 have been negligent supervision and negligent training. Within the scope of vehicular pur-

Table 5.1
ACTING UNDER COLOR OF LAW.

Officers act under the color of law if . . .
1. They identify themselves as a law enforcement agent.
2. They perform duties of a criminal investigation.
3. They file official police documents.
4. They attempt or make an arrest.
5. They invoke their police powers outside their lawful jurisdiction.
6. They settle a personal vendetta with police power.
7. They display or use police weapons/equipment.
8. They act pursuant to a statute or ordinance.
9. The department policy mandates they are "always on duty."
10. They intimidate citizens from exercising their rights.
11. The department supports, facilitates, or encourages the off-duty employment of its officers as private security personnel.

Officers do not act under the color of law if . . .
1. They do not invoke police power.
2. Their inaction does not constitute state action.
3. They commit crimes in a personal dispute without invoking police power.
4. They act as federal agents.
5. They report the details of alleged crimes as private citizens.
6. They work for a private security company and do not identify themselves as law enforcement personnel.
7. The department removes the officers' lawful authority.

suits, the failure to train and supervise are exceedingly important as patrol officers require direction in the execution of proper pursuit procedure.

In a case of failure to supervise, it must be demonstrated that a superior officer, at any step along the hierarchy of command, was negligent in the duty to oversee subordinate performance of official duties in accordance with the law. Liability can be established if a supervisor failed to enforce organizational policy in a regular manner. Supervisors and administrators have the legal obligation to develop and implement departmental procedures and policy. A written manual of all departmental procedures and policies must be disseminated to all officers, accompanied by proper training, to ensure that appropriate legal mandates are met and that officers understand and appreciate the importance of policy and liability (*District of Columbia v. Parker,* 1988).

An allegation of failure to train is a failure of the department to properly provide a subordinate with the skills, training, knowledge, or activities required to adequately perform the tasks incumbent of employment as a police officer. Herein again lies the importance of the development and dissemination of a written departmental policy and procedure manual. Without an adequate training manual, individual officers cannot identify policy and procedural issues the department and the law deem essential to the performance of daily police operations. Very similar to failure to train is failure to direct. The police department has the responsibility of instructing its employees in the specific procedures, conditions, and limits associated with performance of their respective duties. To allow a law enforcement officer to begin the performance of daily duties associated with the position simply serves to increase liability risks for both the officer as well as the department (Carter & Payne, 1988).

CONCLUSION

The field of vehicular pursuits abounds with many important topics of which police administrators must be constantly aware. Researchers continue to develop new, more effective tools, the use of which only serves to strengthen police pursuit policies and protect agencies and officers alike from claims of negligence and liability. Policymakers and administrators must first understand the issues behind claims of liability and negligence as well as the basis behind fundamental policy development. Once the basic building blocks of policy development are understood and appreciated, departmental pursuit policies will offer more protection to civilians, officers, and the agency as a whole.

REFERENCES

Alabama v. Pugh 438 U.S. 781 1978.
Baker v. McCollan, 443 U.S. 137 (1979).

Carter, D. L., & Payne, D. M. (1988). *An evaluation of the Delhi Township police department.* Liability of the police officer and the police organization.

County of Sacramento v. Lewis 98 F.3d 434 1998.

Clapp, J. E. (1996). *Random House legal dictionary.* New York: Random House.

Del Carmen, R. (1991). *Civil liabilities in American policing: A text for law enforcement personnel.* Englewood Cliffs, NJ: Brady.

District of Columbia v. Parker 850 F.2d 1220 1988.

Edelman v. Jordan 415 U.S. 651 1974.

42 U.S.C. § 1983.

Hall, J. C. (1988). Police use of deadly force to arrest: A Constitutional standard. *FBI Law Enforcement Bulletin, 57*(7): 20–29.

Hans v. Louisiana 134 U.S. 1 1890.

Harlow v. Fitzgerald 457 U.S. 800 1982.

Hunter v. Bryant 502 U.S. 224 112 S.Ct. 634 1991.

Jordan v. Kelly 223 F.Supp. 731 1963.

Kappeler, V. E. (2001). *Critical issues in police civil liability* (3rd ed.). Prospect Heights, IL: Waveland Press.

Monell v. Department of Social Services 436 U.S. 658 1978.

Monroe v. Pape 365 U.S. 167 1961.

Oklahoma v. Tuttle 105 S.Ct. 2427 1985.

Parish v. Meyers 226 1924.

Prosser, W. L. (1971). *Handbook of the law of torts* (4th ed.). St. Paul, MN: West.

Roberg, R. R., Kuykendall, J., & Novak, K. (2002). *Police management* (3rd ed.). Los Angeles: Roxbury.

Scheuer v. Rhodes 416 U.S. 232 1974.

Schmidt, W.W. (1976). Recent developments in police civil liability. *Journal of Police Science and Administration, 4:* 197.

Swanson, C. R., Territo, L., & Taylor, R. W. (1993). *Police administration* (3rd ed.). New York: Macmillan.

United States v. Classic 313 U.S. 299 1941.

Vaughn, M. S., & Coomes, L. F. (1995). Police civil liability under Section 1983: When do police officers acts under the color of law? *Journal of Criminal Justice, 23:* 395–415.

Wood v. Strickland 420 U.S. 308 1975.

Worrall, J. L. (1998). Administrative determinants of civil liability lawsuits against municipal police departments: An exploratory analysis. *Crime and Delinquency, 44:* 295–313.

Chapter 6

USE OF FORCE AND VEHICULAR PURSUITS

The profession of policing and law enforcement in the contemporary United States has grown increasingly complex and difficult. Officers face a daily barrage of violence, disrespect, and negative publicity. As academia grows more sophisticated, the realm of policing has become a ripe venue for research and scholarly analysis. Patrol officers now face professional inquiry into their daily operations. Policy and patrol practices have become the focus of scholarly research and investigation. The use of force, liability, administrative practices, and employment policies have been embroiled in controversy and skepticism for many years.

One notable field that remains of interest to academic investigation is police pursuit practices and policies. For many years, police pursuit was viewed as a necessary and vital part of an officer's duty to the public. Law violators were to be apprehended and punished for their infractions. While researchers and police administrators were primarily concerned with policy and liability issues regarding deadly force and community relations, research into the area of pursuits was left to wane. It is only within the past decade that the area of vehicular pursuits has become a topic suitable for scholarly examination. As police liability expands, it has become vital for law enforcement organizations to recognize the importance and significance of viable, legitimate research into the realm of pursuits.

USE OF FORCE

One strategy to understand and appreciate the domain of police pursuits is within the frame of police use of force. In much the same manner that a police firearm is considered an instrument of deadly force, so it is that the patrol cruiser can, at times, be a mechanism of death. As Alpert and Anderson (1986) have stated, ". . . when a police officer engages in a high-speed chase in a high-powered police care, that vehicle becomes a potentially deadly weapon" (p. 2). The myriad of liability and legal issues contained within the sphere of police pursuits are extremely interesting and important to understand for the greater good of society. The argument can also be established that the constitutional arguments developed out of pursuit litigation parallel those generated by instances of police use of force. Many of the same legal tactics and issues inherent in cases of the use of force are utilized in suits alleging liability or negligence in instances of police pursuit. Thus, as the topic of pursuit is of considerable consequence to the field of policing, it is perhaps wise to couch such polemic in the context of the police use of force.

A BRIEF HISTORY OF FORCE

Since the medieval era, deadly force has been utilized by police officers in efforts to apprehend violators of the law. These actions previously were governed by the legal distinction between felony and misdemeanor (Boutwell, 1982). Prior to the modern age of policing, as it has come to be known in the contemporary United States, an officer was justified in using deadly force to prevent the escape of a fleeing felon. Such force, however, was deemed inappropriate or the apprehension of a fleeing misdemeanant (Boutwell, 1982). This, rationale, as iterated by the legal experts of the time, was due to the fact that a felony was punishable by certain death, while a misdemeanant faced only a period of incarceration. An officer's use of deadly force could be explained as merely accelerating the process of bringing a felon to justice. As stated in the case of *Petrie v. Cartwright* (1902), "it made little difference if the suspected felon was killed in the process of capture since, in the eyes of the law, he had already forfeited his life by committing the felony" (p. 299). Instances of fleeing misdemeanants were considered in a more benign light: "To permit the life of one charged with a mere misdemeanor to be taken when fleeing from the officer would, aside from its inhumanity, be productive of more abuse than good. . . . The security of person and property is not endangered by a petty offender being at large" (*Head v. Martin,* 1887, p. 967).

As society developed an increasingly complex justice system, the distinction between felony and misdemeanor became more enigmatic as a larger number of crimes became classified as felonies. As the societal definition and understanding of punishment changed throughout the years, it no longer appeared humane to justify the killing of fleeing felons. Society's collective conscience no longer wholly approved of the use of deadly force in efforts to apprehend fleeing felons. Emil Durkheim underscored the importance of a collective societal response in his famous quote, "We must not say that an action shocks the common conscience because it is criminal, but rather that it is criminal because it shocks the common conscience. We do not reprove it because it is a crime, but it is a crime because we reprove it" (1933, p. 81). Thus, as society grew, so did its perceptions of what could be considered an appropriate police response.

DELIBERATE INDIFFERENCE

The area of deliberate indifference poses some interesting problems for policymakers. Officers need to understand instances where their conduct might endanger the lives of civilians despite the fact that the officer is following proper policy. The field of deliberate indifference has been used by many citizens in an effort to establish or demonstrate police negligence or misconduct.

The first notable case involving a claim of deliberate indifference was that of *Canton v. Harris* (1989). Here, the claim constituted a failure or officers to understand instances when a suspect might genuinely require medical care. The failure of officers to be sensitive to the personal needs of the suspect or prisoner can be a serious source of liability for officers and department alike.

In *Canton v. Harris* (1989), the Supreme Court rejected the contention that a municipality can be held liable under Section § 1983 only if the policy of the municipality was itself unconstitutional. Evidence presented in this case endeavored to demonstrate that the City of Canton, Ohio, had a custom or policy of vesting complete authority with the police supervisor the decision of when medical treatment should be administered to subjects in police custody. It was also maintained by the plaintiff that vesting such authority with police without adequate training to recognize when there was a need for medical assistance was grossly negligent. This ruling required plaintiffs to bridge the gap between policy and injury in a stringent manner. The Court adopted the deliberate indifference standard that was required to be met to establish a constitutional violation by a municipality. This standard has been used by many plaintiffs seeking compensation for instances of police shootings and the use of excessive force. Most of the claims center around a municipality's failure to effectively train its officers so as to avoid the constitutional deprivation (Lewis, 1991).

SUPREME COURT AND FORCE

For a use of force to remain within the boundaries of the law, the officer in question must use only that amount of force that is available to local, state, or federal law enforcement officials. Rather, excessive force is that which exceeds what is deemed reasonable. Contemporary legal authorities rely upon the totality of circumstances in a use of force to make considerations based on the reasonableness of certain police actions. Historically, there have been three suits brought before the United States Supreme Court that have infused the use of force by police with many intricate and significant social issues. The Civil Rights Act of 1964, *Tennessee v. Garner* (1985), and *Graham v. Connor* (1989) have each brought to policing a new understanding of what force is appropriate when analyzing police arrest tactics.

CIVIL RIGHTS ACT 1964

In claims against police alleging instances of willful misconduct or excessive use of force, plaintiffs generally utilize the precepts included within the text of the 1964 Civil Rights Act. A plaintiff may also demonstrate governmental indifference to a wronged party in a suit brought under section 1983 of the Civil Rights Act. Section 1983 has been one of the single most effective tools in bringing claims of liability against governmental entities to suit.

Originally passed in an effort to combat post Civil War activities of the Ku Klux Klan, § 1983 provides that "any person acting under the color of state or local law who violates the federal constitutional or statutory rights of another shall be liable to the injured party" (Alpert & Fridell, 1992, p. 11). Under provisions of § 1983, a plaintiff can attempt to establish governmental indifference that can include allegations of a failure to train, failure to supervise, failure to have a departmental policy, negligent retention, negligent hiring, failure to discipline, failure to screen psychologically, and negligent entrustment (*Canton v. Harris,* 1989). Suits brought under § 1983, rather than alleging violations of the substantive due process clause of the Fourteenth Amendment, constitute claims of an application of excessive force used during an arrest situation (Urbonya, 1987). Thus, incidents in which plaintiffs make claims of excessive force have become events involving questions regarding wrongful or unreasonable seizures rather than due process issues (Urbonya, 1987; *Tennessee v. Garner,* 1985).

As will be explored in subsequent sections, since the Graham decision in 1989, allegations of excessive force are analyzed under the Fourth Amendment and the reasonableness standard (Alpert & Fridell, 1992). Thus, in any § 1983 suit alleging police use of excessive force, the fundamental question becomes one of whether the individual was deprived of a constitutional right through the action or inaction of the officer on the scene (*Tennessee v. Garner,* 1985; *Graham v. Connor,* 1989).

TENNESSEE v. GARNER 1985

The case of *Tennessee v. Garner* (1985) is perhaps the definitive Supreme Court decision regarding police use of force. It has been stated that the Court's ruling in *Tennessee v. Garner* (1985) has had the largest impact on the area of police policy (Lewis, 1991). After a Memphis police officer shot and killed a 15-year-old unarmed burglar fleeing the scene of a residence, a storm of controversy erupted over the officer's actions. The officer on the scene stated that he was reasonably certain the suspect was unarmed but shot to prevent escape. The officer's actions were believed justifiable at the time by existing state law regarding instances of fleeing felons. In the State of Tennessee, police officers were justified in utilizing deadly force to prevent the escape of a fleeing felon. The Court would eventually conclude that the facts surrounding the case did not justify the use of deadly force and that the use of such tactics under the existing circumstances was unreasonable (*Tennessee v. Garner,* 1985).

Originally, the Garner suit alleged violations of the Fourth, Fifth, Sixth, Eighth, and Fourteenth Amendments (Alpert & Fridell, 1992). Upon review, the Sixth Circuit Court of Appeals ruled that the officer's actions amounted to a seizure governed by the provisions of the Fourth Amendment. The Supreme Court would subsequently rule that the officer's actions did, indeed, constitute a seizure applicable to the reasonableness standard of the Fourth Amendment. It was stated by the Court that, although it is not always clear when police interference becomes a seizure, there can be no question that apprehension "by the use of deadly force is a seizure subject to the reasonableness requirement of the Fourth Amendment" (p. 8). The question under analysis concerns the reasonableness of an officer's actions in trying to apprehend a suspect. The Court also stated that, "When an officer restrains the freedom of a person to walk away, he has seized that person" (p. 8). The language of the Court must be carefully scrutinized as later in the same decision it is stated that, "When an officer has probable cause to believe that the suspect poses a threat of serious physical harm, either to the officer or to others, it is not constitutionally unreasonable to prevent escape by using deadly force" (p. 11).

To assist in defining the constitutionality of a seizure, the Court introduced the balancing test. As stated in the Court's conclusion, "The nature and quality of the intrusion on the individual's fourth amendment's interest (must be balanced) against the importance of the governmental interests alleged to justify the intrusion" (*Tennessee v. Garner,* 1985, p. 8, quoting *U.S. v. Place,* 1983, p. 703). In addition, the Court held the Tennessee statute "unconstitutional insofar as it authorizes the use of deadly force against . . . unarmed, nondangerous suspects[s]" (*Tennessee v. Garner,* 1985, p. 11).

The reasonableness standard contained within the Garner decision reads, "Thus, if the suspect threatens the officer with a weapon or there is probable cause to believe that he has committed a crime involving the inflicting or threatened infliction of serious physical harm, deadly force may be used if necessary to prevent escape, and if, where feasible, some warning has been given" (p. 12). Three elements may be gleaned from this single statement: (1) the suspect threatened the officer with a weapon; (2) the officer has probable cause the believe that the suspect has committed a crime involving the infliction or threatened infliction of serious physical harm; and, (3) the officer has given some warning if feasible (Hall, 1988).

These three seemingly simple statements have been at the center of a variety of liability suits with plaintiffs alleging police used improper force when attempting to apprehend a suspect. The presence of a weapon in the hands of suspects has been dealt with in a fairly concise manner. The Court states, "Without question an officer can use deadly force in the immediate defense of his life or the lives of others" (Hall, 1988, p. 4). However, the Court also stated that such action by a suspect can justify the officer's use of deadly force to prevent escape due to the fact that the individual poses an obvious danger to the community at large.

A case in point illustrating this very position is that of *Crawford v. Edmonson* (1985). The case, in brief, centered around the officer, Edmonson, firing at the main suspect, known to be armed, but accidentally hitting the second suspect. The Court reasoned that the second unarmed suspect was not an innocent bystander, but rather a willing participant in an armed robbery. In concluding, the Court noted that there was "sufficient evidence that Edmonson did what a reasonably careful person would have done under the circumstances"(Hall, 1988, p. 5).

Another case illustrating the importance of the presence of a weapon is that of *Amato v. United States* (1982). In this case, one bank robbery suspect sued the U.S. government for wounds suffered from FBI agents in a shootout that was triggered by a second suspect's firing at federal agents. The plaintiff contended that he was in the process of surrendering to agents when the battle began and he was wounded. The Court observed, "If [one's co-conspirator] has used deadly force against police officers, and they reasonably fear that he ill continue to do so, the one is inclined to surrender may be unable to dissolve his association where his partner, in close proximity, appears to have plans to carry on the battle. Having determined to enter into an illegal enterprise, the plaintiff may have deprived himself of the right and ability to disassociate himself from the venture under such circumstances" (p. 869).

One last case used to highlight the intricacies involved in any incident involving the use of deadly force by police is *O'Neal v. DeKalb County* (1987). Here, officers shot and killed a hospital patient who had stabbed six people. The family of the perpetrator sued the officers, their superiors, and the county government alleging violations of numerous constitutional provisions, including the Fourth Amendment. The plaintiffs contended, inter alia, that O'Neal was not in the process of attacking the officers but was intent on escape. The court did not attempt to resolve the factual issues under dispute but held that even if O'Neal was trying to escape, the use of deadly force under the circumstances was not unconstitutional (Hall, 1988).

The third statement of the reasonableness requirement of the Garner decision has also been closely scrutinized by the courts. This portion of the reasonableness standard concerns the issue of a warning, if feasible, provided by the officer to the suspect prior to using deadly force. It has been stated that the requirement is consistent with the common law notion that deadly force should only be used when necessary. The Court has also noted that, ". . . even a criminal in the course of committing a crime has certain rights. If he surrenders upon command, does not resist, and makes no attempt to flee, he cannot and should not be physically harmed, no matter how serious the crime just committed may be" (*Amato v. United States*, 1982, p. 869).

In *Hill v. Jenkins* (1985), the plaintiff contended that the decision in Garner requires an officer to give a specific warning prior to shooting, apparently suggesting that a shouted command to halt is insufficient. Although conceding that the Garner decision requires some warning where feasible before deadly force is applied, the Court rejected the idea that more is required than a shouted command to stop or halt (Hall, 1988).

GRAHAM v. CONNOR 1989

The case of *Graham v. Connor* (1989) is relevant to the use of force by police in establishing the totality of circumstances in instances of a use of force allegation. In Graham, the plaintiff, a diabetic, alleged excessive force was used after an officer observed what he considered suspicious activity in a convenience store. Graham had entered the store in an effort to purchase orange juice to stave off an oncoming insulin reaction. Upon deciding that the line of customers was too long, the plaintiff opted, instead, to travel to a friend's house to get the needed juice. The officer became more suspicious, requested backup, and halted the car driven by Graham's friend. After exiting the car,

Graham was handcuffed, placed on the hood of the vehicle, and in the ensuing confusion suffered a broken foot, bruised forehead, a shoulder injury, and continues to suffer from ringing in the ears (*Graham v. Connor,* 1989). Graham brought suit under § 1983, alleging the officer used excessive force in the investigatory stop.

After review by the Fourth Circuit Court of Appeals, a decision by a lower court was affirmed stating that the amount of force used in the case was not excessive. However, upon appeal, the Supreme Court reversed that decision ruling that the lower courts had applied an incorrect legal standard (Kappeler, 1993). Lower courts had applied a substantive due process standard based on Fourteenth Amendment considerations (Urbonya, 1987). The Supreme Court ruled that an incorrect decision and applied, instead, the Fourth Amendment's objective reasonableness standard (Urbonya, 1987). To iterate the point, the Court stated, "all claims that law enforcement officers have used excessive force-deadly or not-in the course of an arrest, investigatory stop, or other 'seizure' of a free citizen should be analyzed under the 4th Amendment and its [objective] 'reasonableness' standard" (*Graham v. Connor,* 1989, p. 1871).

The objective reasonableness standard consists of a two-part rule. The first consideration consists of a warning against the use of subjective interpretations in suits alleging excessive force (Kappeler, 1993). Upon review of Graham, the Court rejected the former substantive due process standard in favor of a more objective stance concerning an examination of facts surrounding the case. Therefore, no longer were defendants required to prove that officers acted in a sadistic or malicious manner in applications of force in arrest situations. Subsequent decisions would be made without regard to the officer's intent or motivation. Decisions would be shaped "from the perspective of a reasonable officer on the scene, rather than with the 20/20 vision of hindsight" (*Graham v. Connor,* 1989, p. 1872). Additionally, the Court's ruling considers the totality of the circumstances surrounding an event, "The question is whether the totality of the circumstances justified a particular sort of . . . seizure" (p. 396).

The second consideration of Graham concerns the reasonableness of a particular seizure (Alpert & Fridell, 1992). The reasonableness of a seizure can be understood simply as an application of the balancing test of Garner (Alpert & Fridell, 1992). Additional factors enter into the decision due to the fact that the decision of Graham did not constitute an instance of the use of deadly force, as was the case in Garner. The Court stated that, "the test of reasonableness under the Fourth Amendment is not capable of precise definition or mechanical application, however, its proper application requires careful attention to the facts and circumstances of each particular case, including the severity of the crime at issue, whether the suspect poses an immediate threat to the safety of the officer or others, and whether he is actively resisting or attempting to evade arrest by flight" (*Graham v. Connor,* 1989, p. 1871, quoting *Bell v. Wolfish,* 1979, p. 559). Hence, additional factors must, by necessity, be considered.

Here the Court considered four factors in determining when the use of force was excessive. The factors, "to be considered in determining when the excessive use of force gives rise to a cause of action under § 1983: 1) the need for the application of force; 2) the relationship between that need and the amount of force that was used; 3) the extent of the injury inflicted, and; 4) whether the force was applied in a good faith effort to maintain and restore discipline or maliciously, and sadistically for the very purpose of causing harm" (p. 391).

ROAD BLOCKS

One important area in which police engage in efforts to stop fleeing suspects centers around the use of roadblocks. In *Stanulonis v. Marzec* (1986), the court declined to dismiss a suit against three officers who had been engaged in an attempt to stop a fleeing motorist. In efforts to stop the speeding motorcycle, one officer parked his patrol car perpendicular to the road, eventually resulting in a collision and death of the cyclist. In declining to dismiss the suit, the court held that, "if proven to be true, the officer's movement of the car to the center of the road when the plaintiff was so close as to create an immediate risk of a collision and significant injury" could constitute "unreasonable force in an attempt to apprehend plaintiff" (p. 1545). Thus, the Stanulonis case should be read and understood by administrators to mean that a roadblock is a seizure subject to the Fourth Amendment.

In a similar case, *Brower v. Inyo County* (1987), a roadblock was established to stop a suspect in an auto theft. The prime difference between the Brower roadblock and that erected by the officer in the Stanulonis case centered upon the distance between the blockage and the fleeing suspect. Officers in the Brower case provided the suspect ample time to notice the roadblock and come to a halt before the impending collision. However, the suspect failed to stop and was killed in the resulting crash. In the ensuing lawsuit, the appellate court held that Brower had, in fact, not been seized by the officers in question. The decision was later explained by the court, "Although Brower was stopped in the literal sense by his impact with the roadblock, he was not 'seized' by the police in the constitutional sense. Prior to his failure to stop voluntarily, his freedom of movement was never arrested or restrained. He had a number of opportunities to stop his automobile prior to the impact" (p. 546).

USE OF FORCE AND POLICY

As administrators and policymakers strive to identify issues of liability, it is their next responsibility to understand the areas inherent in a more encompassing policy. Departmental orders or directives should become a standard part of every law enforcement organization. Specific departmental orders and directives form the administrative foundation upon which the organization rests. Without a firm foundation, eventually an organization will become a target for liability and negligence suits. The administrative foundation of a department must specify the parameters of organizational behavior through policies, procedures, and rules or regulations. Authority, responsibility, and duties are each rung of the hierarchical ladder if contained in departmental policy (Carter, 1986).

In light of the recent litigation, it is imperative that each police department, no matter how small, have a precise, written, comprehensive, and substantively strong policy and directives. Administrators and policymakers must be aware of the differences in terminology of the specific directives contained in the composition of the policy. Policy, objectives, procedures, rules, general orders, special orders, memoranda, and written directives are each unique entities unto themselves and each provides a small portion of the larger departmental directive.

Once administrators and policymakers are adept at recognizing when an issue might pose a problem of negligence or liability, it is necessary to consider the methods by which the new policy is to be dis-

seminated to officers in the department. Administrators must acknowledge the importance of the use of training, supervision, evaluation,
and guidance when presenting officers with policy.

Additionally, it is incumbent upon administrators to place constraints upon officers' use of force. The incorporation of a use of force
continuum in policy is one technique to curtail unrestrained uses of
force by officers. There are numerous use of force continuums available for a department to utilize in its use of force policy. A department
should critically evaluate a use of force continuum, examining the
model to determine if it is easily understandable and easily recalled by
officers under stressful circumstances. It is also necessary for a department to incorporate a statement into the policy dealing with such
issues as officer age, size, gender, strength, skill, injury, and exhaustion. A strong affirmative stance by the department will provide officers with confidence and support when trying to make decision in the
field (O'Linn, 1992).

Due to the fact that the use of force does not occur in a vacuum, it
is imperative that officers be properly trained in the use of force techniques as a separate entity. Many departments train officers in defense
techniques in a static environment. Recruits never experience a realistic training scenario. Thus, it is vital that training in the use of force be
as realistic as possible. This allows officers an opportunity to evaluate
their own understanding of the department's policies regarding force.
Areas of potential difficulties for officers in the field include handcuffing suspects, transporting prisoners, searching suspects, extracting suspects from vehicles, and making arrests following pursuits (O'Linn,
1992).

Not only is it imperative for line officers to be properly trained, it is
also important for supervisory personnel to understand and appreciate
the training that such officers receive. Frequently, supervisory and
administrative personnel fail to continue with updated hands-on training. The result of this neglect by administrators and supervisors is not
only a loss of technical expertise, but a loss of understanding concerning this fundamental portion of a field training officer's (FTO's) duty. As
stated by O'Linn (1992), "FTO's must possess a thorough understanding of current use-of-force training and policy as it was provided to
recent graduates of the police academy, since new officers look to the
FTO for guidance on implementing their new skills" (p. 53).

One potential result of the lack of administrators' continued training is a failure to consistently judge instances of the use of force by officers in the field. Without the same training as field officers, administrators and supervisors may not evaluate a situation in the same manner as officers who were trained by departmental instructors. The consequence of differing evaluation schema can be a dichotomy between rules followed by line officers and those adhered to by administrators. This inconsistency leads only to confusion and morale problems. It may also lead to hesitancy by officers in the field, public distrust of the department, and increased liability exposure for the organization and its employees (O'Linn, 1992).

To lessen the risk of liability, a periodic review of use-of-force incidents may indicate a trend within the organization. Analyzing use-of-force incidents in terms of various techniques employed, devices used, individual problems, an indication of officers' misunderstanding policy, lack of confidence, or lack of self-control is prudent for administrators seeking ways to lessen potential liability risks for the organization.

Officers also require guidance concerning the proper understanding of the department's use-of-force policy. Officers are required to be split-second decision-makers and they depend upon the guidance and supervision of the training officers to provide them with the confidence and comprehension to act with deliberation and speed. The law enforcement agency needs to provide its officers with precise and consistent appraisal during training and evaluation.

CONCLUSION

The duties required of police officers arise from various sources: law, custom, judicial decisions, and departmental policy. Police officers have a duty to protect the citizenry from unnecessary and unreasonable harm while simultaneously pursuing and apprehending law violators. The legal duty of protection and breach of that duty can place officers and departments alike at risk for claims of liability and negligence. Administrators must caution officers to proceed with due care whenever engaging in pursuit of a violator.

It is evident that the creation of policy with regard to pursuits is a complicated, analytical process. Administrators and policymakers must be aware of current liability trends, tort law, federal civil rights law, negligibility requirements, and liability issues. These legal details must then be incorporated into a concise, available, and comprehensible policy. Officers must be thoroughly trained on the proper use of force and the implications for improper conduct in the field. As administrators develop and implement policy, they lessen any chances of subsequent liability or negligence suits from becoming reality.

REFERENCES

42 U.S.C. § 1983.

Alpert, G.P., & Anderson, P. (1986). The most deadly force: Police pursuits. *Justice Quarterly, 3,* 1–14.

Alpert, G., & Fridell, L. (1992). *Police vehicles and firearms.* Prospect Heights, IL: Waveland Press.

Amato v. United States 549 F.Supp. 863 D. N.J. 1982.

Bell v. Wolfish 441 U.S. 520 1979.

Boutwell, J. P. (1982). Use of deadly force to arrest a fleeing felon-A Constitutional challenge, Part I. *FBI Law Enforcement Bulletin, 46*(9): 27–31.

Brower v. County of Inyo, 489 U.S. 593 (1989).

Canton v. Harris, 109 S.Ct. 1197 (1989).

Carter, D. L. (1986). *Police deviance.* Cincinnati, OH: Anderson.

Crawford v. Edmonson 764 F.2d 479, 7th Cir. 1985.

Durkheim, E. (1933). *The division of labor in society.* New York: Free Press.

Graham v. Connor, 490 U.S. 386 (1989).

Hall, J.C. (1988). Police use of deadly force to arrest: A Constitutional standard. *FBI Law Enforcement Bulletin, 57*(7): 20–29.

Head v. Martin, 3 S.W. 622, 623 (Ky. Ct. App. 1887).

Hill v. Jenkins 620 F. Supp. 853 N.D. Ga. 1987.

Kappeler, V. E. (1993). *Critical issues in police liability.* Prospect Heights, IL: Waveland Press.

Lewis, K. L. (1991). Section 1983: A matter of policy-current overview of municipal liability. *Michigan Bar Journal,* June: 556–559.

O'Linn, M. K. (1992). The gaps in the use-of-force policies and training. *The Police Chief,* February: 52–54.

O'Neal v. DeKalb County 667 F. Supp. 272 N.D. Ill. 1985.

Petrie v. Cartwright, 70 S.W. 297, 299 (Ky., 1902).

Stanulonis v. Marzec 649 F. Supp. 1536 D. Conn. (1986).

Tennessee v. Garner, 471 U.S. 1 (1985).

Urbonya, K. (1987). Establishing a deprivation of a constitutional right to personal safety under Section 1983: The use of unjustified force by state officials in violation of the Fourth, Eighth, and Fourteenth Amendments. *Albany Law Review, 51:* 171–235.

United States v. Place 617 F.Supp. 1015 (D.C. Cal.) 1985.

Chapter 7

NATIONAL PURSUIT POLICY, TECHNOLOGICAL PROPOSALS, AND LEGISLATIVE ADVANCEMENTS

As is evident by viewing any weeknight television news program, police vehicular pursuits continue to pose dilemmas for police agencies, political figureheads, civil rights organizations, and the public in general. Police are placed time and time again in the awkward and unique position of endeavoring to apprehend a law violator or a known fugitive without placing in peril the lives of innocent members of the general public. A reckless, dangerous, or negligent pursuit can place innocent civilians in danger. However, a failure to successfully apprehend a suspect ultimately means that the general public is still placed in harms way due to the at-large nature of the suspect. Therein lies the crux of the problem, the catch 22. The fundamental argument remains that the duty of the police is to protect, not harm.

The myriad of issues surrounding police pursuits is replete with concerns regarding liability, negligence, force, reporting, and community relations. As litigation continues to grow the Constitutional issues raised by Fourth and Fourteenth Amendment considerations also plague many law enforcement agencies. Apart from considerations pertaining to departmental liability, there also exists the very real issue of monetary compensations concerning pursuits. Litigation resulting from tragic outcomes of vehicular pursuits can easily grow into the millions of dollars annually. Taxpayers and police agencies suffer equally when a pursuit goes awry and a claim of negligence or liability is substantiated. Thus, it is vital for a law enforcement agency to have in effect a viable, trainable vehicular pursuit policy to serve as a guide for officer discretion while in the field. A comprehensive policy acts as a guide for officer discretion so they can better choose a more mindful course of action while conducting a pursuit.

In any decision to engage in a vehicular pursuit, the need to apprehend the suspect must be weighed against the need to avoid endangering civilians or other parties not directly involved in the ongoing pursuit. Generally, the greater the potential risk to the general public, the officer, or the suspect, the less justified the pursuit. While it is impractical, and perhaps illogical, to formulate precise, objective rules to cover the many complexities of a pursuit, it is, nonetheless, vital for an agency to develop a comprehensive policy governing the conduct of officers while in the midst of a vehicular pursuit.

As administrators and policymakers finish in their task to relate policy to issues of liability, it is their next responsibility to understand the many areas inherent in a well encompassing policy. Departmental orders or directives should become a standard part of every law enforcement organization. Specific departmental orders and directives form the administrative foundation upon which the organization rests. Without a firm foundation, eventually an organization will become a target for liability and negligence suits. The administrative foundation of a department must specify the parameters of organizational behavior through policies, procedures, and rules or regulations. Authority, responsibility, and duties of each rung of the hierarchical ladder are contained in departmental policy (Carter, 1986).

In light of the recent trend of litigation, it is imperative that each police department, no matter how small, have a precise, written, comprehensive, and substantively strong policy and directives. Administrators and policymakers must be aware of the differences in terminology of the specific directives contained in the composition of the policy. Policy, objectives, procedures, rules, general orders, special orders, memoranda, and written directives are each unique entities unto themselves and each provide a small portion of the larger departmental directive.

As per policy development, any law enforcement agency should have in effect a vehicular pursuit policy inclusive of any elements pertaining to deadly force or potentially hazardous forcible stop techniques. The omission of even a single element pertaining to the safety of the pursuing officer, suspect, pedestrians, or innocent third parties has far reaching Fourth and Fourteenth Amendment consequences.

Deadly force and negligence suits can have devastating financial reper-
cussions for law enforcement agencies, not to mention the personal and
career toll placed upon an officer or victim of a pursuit gone awry.

A failure to include potentially hazardous elements into a pursuit
policy serves to increase the dangerousness factor inherent in any pursuit and raises the stakes on the gamble with human life, property, and
the possibility of negligence and liability claims.

Some of the earliest research into police vehicular pursuits was often
sensational lacking the strict scientific methodological guidelines that
direct current scholarly endeavors. One of the earliest research projects into the field of vehicular pursuits was the Physicians for
Automotive Safety (1968). Unfortunately, this study was utilized more
in courts of law by unscrupulous attorneys seeking monetary rewards
for their clients than by scholars seeking a serious study of the police
role in society. Many years and research projects later, modern scholars would begin to appreciate and understand the importance of police
pursuits in the larger realm of law enforcement and policing.

While many arguments espoused by proponents and opponents of
vehicular pursuits remain emotionally charged, many scholars and legislators have acknowledged the importance of this specific law enforcement function. Despite evidence to the contrary there still exist those
scholars and community leaders who maintain that police pursuits pose
too many inherent risks to the general public and innocent bystanders.
Were it not for police pursuits, many suspects would be let loose on an
unsuspecting public. In a 1993 study by Payne of police pursuits in the
State of Michigan, it was reported that the majority of pursuits were initiated for speeding (30.5%), followed by other traffic violations (24.9%)
and suspected felony crimes (24.3%). Upon apprehension of the suspect, Payne found that 34.5 percent of the pursuits resulted in an arrest
involving a felony, 33.1 percent involved a charge of fleeing and eluding, with 14.4 percent involving drunk driving charges.

In an earlier study by Alpert and Dunham (1988) of pursuits by the
Metro Dade Police Department and the Miami Police Department, it
was discovered that out of a total 952 pursuits, 47 percent (n = 305) of
apprehended suspects were arrested for traffic violations and 48 percent
(n = 314) were arrested for felonies. Were it not for the practice of police
vehicular pursuits, dangerous felons would be free to run amok in society. Charles, Falcone, and Wells (1992a) obtained results in their study
of pursuits indicating that 95.9 percent of all officers interviewed voiced

approval for pursuits. They also found that 76.3 percent of officers indicated that they believed that the danger to the public would increase if
their department were to halt all pursuits, while 85.4 percent maintained
that crime in general would increase (Charles et al., 1992a). Finally,
Britz and Payne (1994) observed that, "An overwhelming majority of
respondents (96%) supported the notion that more offenders would
attempt to elude police if such a policy were implemented" (p. 117).
Thus, it would seem, as far as the officers themselves are concerned, the
law enforcement tactic of vehicular pursuits is highly supported.

REGIONAL VARIATIONS

Some theorists have espoused the idea of a nationwide pursuit policy. Although the chances of this actually occurring in the near future
are remote, it is, nonetheless, a topic worthy of consideration.

Due to the vast expanse of the United States, the effort to standard-
ize vehicular pursuit policies is ultimately doomed to failure. It is an
exercise in futility. The United States is a country of differing geogra-
phy, population densities, and cultures. What is appropriate for one
state could prove to be highly inappropriate for another. For example,
what would be successful and appropriate in the megalopolis of the
Eastern Seaboard would not be necessary or even desirable in a large,
sparsely populated western state.

A densely populated region covering a small geographic area is in
need of a highly articulated pursuit policy detailing various potentially hazardous pursuit tactics. In efforts to apprehend fleeing suspects
while maintaining safety for the general public, a detailed, comprehensive policy is a must. Although the policy serves merely as a guide
to officer discretion, it, nevertheless, offers some protection against
foolhardy tactics and aids the officer in choosing a safe, effective
course of action.

Conversely, in a sparsely populated region covering a large square
mile area an intensively detailed policy is, in all likelihood, not necessary. While the policy should be comprehensive enough to allow for
dangerous tactics and maneuvers, it is not necessary or desirable for
an organization to create a pursuit policy that is so profoundly detailed
that it tries to cover every possible scenario an officer could experience. This simply creates added anxiety on the part of the officer as

unessential information is placed into memory.

The culture of a specific area is also a factor that must be considered when broaching the topic of vehicular pursuit policies. The culture of the eastern portion of the United States is one of long-standing accommodation to matters pertaining to law and public administration (Johnson, Aldrich, Miller, Ostrom, & Rhode, 1990). This is where American government was born. Citizens and law enforcement officials are accustomed to the requirements of bureaucracies and administration. As stated previously, it is in this relatively small geographic area with a dense population that an intensively detailed pursuit policy would be most appropriate. As the population density increased, so, too, would the opportunity for danger to arise during the course of a vehicular pursuit. A more comprehensive pursuit policy could bring an added measure of safety to an already dangerous situation.

Nevertheless, a comprehensive vehicular pursuit policy is a must for any and all law enforcement agencies. However, the form this policy is to take can vary considerably from department to department. If the policy contains all of the relevant safeguards pertaining to high-speed driving and dangerous tactics such as ramming, roadblocks, shooting, or boxing-in, it would probably suffice for that area. As in any other area, the policy serves to guide officer discretion and protects the agency and officer from unsubstantiated claims of liability and negligence.

In a study by Hicks (2001), written vehicular pursuit policies of state police agencies across the nation were compared and analyzed based on their respective inclusiveness and comprehensiveness on a variety of factors. Due to the vast differences existing across the United States, a thorough examination of state police policies will provide some insight into the applicability or feasibility of a nationwide pursuit policy. Difficulties with providing an appropriate level of comprehensiveness in a national policy have already been discussed. State police policies are the best representation of police practices in vastly differing regions nationwide.

Due to the fact that police pursuits involve both tactical as well as administrative elements, each of the statements included in the state police policies were divided into administrative and operational factors. Table 7.1 below outlines the factors gleaned from the analysis of state police written vehicular pursuit policies. A thoroughly comprehensive policy would contain all of the Administrative and Operational factors listed in this table.

Table 7.1.

Administrative	Operational
1. Mission Statement	1. Initiate Pursuit
2. Safety Caveat	2. Notify Dispatcher/Supervisor
3. Discontinuance of Pursuit	3. Specifics of Pursuit Conditions
4. Noncompliance	4. Provisions for Lights & Sirens
5. Definitions	5. Tactical Considerations
6. Authority to Pursue	6. Jurisdictional Considerations
7. Statutory Duties	7. Pursuit Driving
8. Case Law References	8. Caravaning
9. Pursuit Restrictions	9. Intentional Collisions
10. Seriousness of Offense	10. Shooting from Vehicle
11. Role of Dispatch	11. Unmarked Car/Motorcycle
12. Requirement of Supervisor to Monitor	12. Boxing-in
13. Role of Supervisor	13. Heading Off/Passing
14. Training	14. Paralleling
15. Supervisor at Termination Point	15. Roadblocks
16. Report Requirements	16. Speed
17. Debriefing	17. Passengers
18. Role of Pursuing Officer	18. Tire Deflation Devices
	19. Off-Road Pursuit
	20. Termination of Pursuit/Reinstating Pursuit
	21. Aerial Assistance

It is important to note that the vast majority of state agencies' pursuit policies contained references to safety. It is pertinent to state here that of the nation's 50 state police agencies, only 47 were willing to participate in this study due to a variety of legal concerns raised by the respective administrators. The Administrative element of Safety Caveat was contained within the text of 47 (100%) of the agencies' policies. Discontinuance of Pursuit, which can also relate to the safety of officers, third parties, and suspects, was included in 41 (87.23%) policies. Pursuit Restrictions, also pertaining to safety-related functions during a vehicular pursuit, was included in 45 (95.74%) of the state policies. Seriousness of Offense, which can pose Fourth Amendment issues, was contained in 40 (85.11%) of the state policies. Finally, Training, which can increase safety during a pursuit and limit officer and agency liability, was included in only 13 (27.66%). Therefore, it can be seen from the above simple frequencies that the majority of state police agencies had elements pertaining to safety included within the text of their respective written pursuit policies.

When analyzing the Operational elements, safety was again the primary consideration. The elements of Intentional Collisions, Shooting from a Vehicle, Boxing-in, Heading-Off/Passing, Paralleling, Roadblocks, and Speed were believed to pose the most danger to the pursuing officer, suspect(s), and general public. These factors also pose important Fourth and Fourteenth Amendment liability risks for a department. While safety has been emphasized by the inclusion of the majority of Administrative elements serving to diminish the potential dangerousness of a pursuit, many Operational elements serving a similar function failed to be included in many state policies. It was observed that only 30 (63.83%) of the state agencies contained the element of Intentional Collisions in their pursuit policies. The factor of Shooting from a Vehicle was included in 29 (61.70%) of the policies. Boxing-in was included in 12 (25.53%) of the state policies. Heading-Off/Passing was contained in 12 (25.53%) of the policies. Paralleling was included in 12 (25.53%) of the policies, Roadblocks was contained in 36 (76.60%) of the policies, and Speed was included in 20 (42.55%). Finally, Termination of Pursuit was included in 46 (97.87%) of the state policies.

Regional analyses can shed even more light on the possibility or feasibility of a national pursuit policy. It was observed that state police agencies of the Northeast and Midwest regions of the United States have the most comprehensive written pursuit policies of any areas of the nation. These two regions of the nation are home to large urban areas with high population densities. More comprehensive written pursuit policies are a necessary feature of police operations in areas with highly congested population densities. Safety of the motoring public is essential as is the protection of patrol officers and law enforcement agencies from unsubstantiated claims of liability or negligence.

It was also observed that the Mountain and Pacific regions of the nation failed to include many of the Administrative factors in their written pursuit policies. It must be remembered that these two regions of the nation do not have the population density or large urban areas that are found in the Northeast and Midwest. Intricate or thoroughly comprehensive written policies might not be required of police officers patrolling primarily rural territory. While safety of the general public is always essential to effective and efficient police operations in sparsely populated regions, a highly detailed written policy is simply not required to enhance the safety of the citizenry.

In an effort to gain additional insight into the consequences of liability and negligence risks for law enforcement agencies, Hicks (2001) divided the Operational factors into two categories: Contextual and Active elements. This distinction was based primarily upon the nature of the respective factor. Contextual Operational elements were those factors inherent in the surrounding environment of the pursuit. These elements did not contain any potentially dangerous forcible stop techniques or driving maneuvers. Characteristics of the circumstances surrounding the pursuit such as Initiate Pursuit, Notify Dispatch, Specifics of Pursuit Conditions, Jurisdictional Considerations, Unmarked Car/Motorcycle, Passengers, Off-Road Pursuit, and Aerial Assistance were all considered contextual Operational elements. All other Operational elements were grouped under the active category. These elements contained all forcible stop techniques and potentially dangerous maneuvers.

It was observed that the pursuit policies of all of the state agencies contained 62.32 percent, an average of 6.02 of the Active Operational elements. The vehicular pursuit policies of states in the Pacific region contained 56.92 percent, an average of 2.85 of the Active Operational elements. Policies of states in the Northeast region included 64.34 percent, an average of 7.08 of the Active Operational elements. Written vehicular pursuit policies of agencies in the Mountain region included 56.04 percent, an average of 3.92 of the Active Operational elements. Policies in the South region contained 61.54 percent, an average of 6.77 of the Active Operational elements. Finally, the states in the Midwest region included 72.78 percent, an average of 9.46 of the Active Operational elements in their written vehicular pursuit policies.

It can be observed again that the state agencies of the Pacific and Mountain regions have the least comprehensive written policies of any region in the nation. Although the argument can be made that highly detailed written policies might not be necessary, or even desired when analyzing Administrative factors, it is a different story altogether when Active Operational elements are concerned. Factors inherent in a vehicular pursuit containing any reference to safety should, by necessity, be included in the written pursuit policies of any law enforcement agency. While an all-encompassing nationwide pursuit policy might not be a necessary condition for safe and effective law enforcement, elements associated with safety need to be included in any written pursuit policy. This serves to protect the general public, the pursuing officer, the suspect, and the department as a whole.

Results indicated that the written pursuit policies of the state agencies contained 64.44 percent, an average of 6.25 of the Contextual Operational elements. The vehicular pursuit policies of states in the Pacific region contained 47.50 percent, an average of 2.375 of the Contextual Operational elements. Policies of states in the Northeast region included 67.05 percent, an average of 7.375 of the Contextual Operational elements. Written vehicular pursuit policies of agencies in the Mountain region included 69.64 percent, an average of 4.875 of the Contextual Operational elements. Policies in the South region contained 65.91 percent, an average of 7.25 of the Contextual Operational elements. Finally, the states in the Mountain region included 72.12 percent, an average of 9.375 of the Contextual Operational elements in their written vehicular pursuit policies.

As is evident in the description of the work conducted by Hicks (2001), each region has its own distinct law enforcement needs. While a uniform, national pursuit policy might not be required to satisfy every legal need to provide safety to the general public and protection from unnecessary danger so often associated with pursuit conditions, some general policy reform might, nonetheless be beneficial to all parties concerned. While some rural states do not require a highly detailed or intricate written policy, improvement in areas such as dangerous forcible stop techniques might provide agencies with added protection from risks of liability or negligence. Additional training for patrol officers is also one method by which to increase safety and add a small measure of protection from unnecessary risks of liability or negligence.

FACTOR ANALYSIS

In addition to basic descriptive statistics, a factor analysis, was conducted in an effort to determine the most important element included in any pursuit-related policy. In the factor analysis of the Administrative elements, six factors were extracted in a Varimax Rotation utilizing a Kaiser Normalization. Factor loadings on each of the administrative elements can be seen in Table 7.2.

It should be noted that the element of Safety Caveat was not included in the factor model. This element had zero variance, and, therefore, would not fit into any factor analytic model. Due to its zero variance, it was decided to remove the element from the larger model and create a separate component entitled "Safety" specifically for this single element.

Table 7.2.

Element	Training	Legal	Mission	Compliance	Restrictions	Roles
1. Mission Statement	–	–	.802	–	–	–
2. Discontinuance of Pursuit	–	–	–	.609	–	–
3. Noncompliance	–	–	–	.754	–	–
4. Definitions	–	–	–	–	–	.607
5. Authority to Pursue	–	.714	–	–	–	–
6. Statutory Duties	–	–	–	–	.486	–
7. Case Law References	–	.759	–	–	–	–
8. Pursuit Restrictions	–	–	–	–	.736	–
9. Seriousness of Offense	–	–	.617	–	–	–
10. Role of Dispatch	–	–	–	–	–	.797
11. Requirement of Supervisor to Monitor	–	–	–	–	–	.531
12. Role of Supervsior	–	–	–	–	–	.648
13. Training	.883	–	–	–	–	–
14. Supervisor at Termination Point	–	–	–	–	–	.150
15. Report Requirements	–	–	–	–	–	.802
16. Debriefing	–	–	–	–	–	.532
Mean	.883	.737	.710	.682	.611	.581

After a review of the individual factor loadings, several primary components became clear. Depending upon the nature and purpose of any particular element, the components were named accordingly. For example, the factor loadings for Component 1 were highest on elements Definitions, Role of Dispatch, Requirement of Supervisor to Monitor, Role of Supervisor, Supervisor at Termination Point, Report Requirements, and Debriefing. This Component was referred to as "Roles" due to the characteristics of each element loading under this component. Each element loading under Component 1 had some reference to the role the person in question was to play according to departmental regulations. All other components were named according to their nature. Therefore, the Administrative elements can be grouped according to seven categories: Roles, Restrictions, Mission, Compliance, Legal, Training, and Safety.

While exploratory factor analysis cannot determine any precise causation, deduction combined with the information provided by the mathematical mock-up can offer guidance in determining which elements dominate. Administratively, the elements pertaining to safety were, by far, the most included of any element. This element had zero variance in the factor model. Thus, Safety should be preeminent in any written pursuit policy. This element could be considered the most important Administrative element.

When trying to determine which factors should be included in a highly comprehensive written policy an examination of the factor loadings would certainly help. The elements should appear in a written pursuit policy in the order of importance indicated by the factor loading model. Therefore, elements dedicated to Safety should be of paramount importance in a written policy followed in order by the elements pertaining to Training, Legal, Mission, Compliance, Restrictions, and Roles.

LEGISLATIVE ANALYSIS

In an effort to lessen the exposure of law enforcement organizations to claims of negligence and liability, several states have devised the strategy of implementing legal standards to be included in a vehicular pursuit policy. If a law enforcement agency is to retain statutory immunity in a court of law in suits alleging liability or officer negligence, certain specified elements must be included in the vehicular pursuit policy. Recently this trend has been expanding nationwide as state legislatures realize the monetary gain inherent in limiting police liability. Apart from monetary considerations ,the increased safety factor from a more comprehensive policy is also a public relations boon for both the agency as well as the legislators themselves.

As the trend of statewide pursuit policies continues to be accepted, the importance of safety is never so evident. Each state bill or law outlines the necessity for a pursuing officer to balance the importance of apprehending the suspect against the risks to the public, themselves, and the suspect. As the statewide policies are designed to limit a department's exposure to claims of liability and negligence an emphasis on safety is logical. If the risks to the public or the officer outweigh the necessity to apprehend the suspect, then continuing with the pursuit is not justified and further pursuit action should be terminated.

Currently, the states of California, Minnesota, and Connecticut have implemented legal standards dictating essential elements to be included by the law enforcement organization in their respective states. In 1985, the state of New Jersey created the New Jersey Police Vehicular Pursuit Policy to be used as a statewide standard for all departments within the state. This standard was revised in January, 1993 and again in September, 1999, but the state legislature has yet to specify the necessity that this standard be implemented into actual law. It is important to note that the definition devised by the New Jersey Task Force is used by the majority of state agencies in defining a police pursuit.

In 1997, the state of Connecticut enacted House Bill No. 5186, An Act Concerning Legislative Task Forces. This bill established a task force similar in duty to that of New Jersey. This task force consisted of two members appointed by the speaker of the house, two appointed by the president pro tempore of the Senate, one appointed by the majority leader of the House, one appointed by the majority leader of the Senate, two appointed by the minority leader of the House, and two appointed by the minority leader of the Senate. The task force was assigned the duty to "study the feasibility of a standardized, unified police pursuit policy within the state" (p. 1). The report from the task force was to be submitted no later than January 1, 1998 to the joint standing committee of the General Assembly. Again, the bill stated the importance of safety in the task forces report and the possibility of a statewide, uniform pursuit policy.

The state of Minnesota, in Minnesota Statute § 609.487 (1999), legally defined the variety of terms and conditions existing within the scope of a police vehicular pursuit. This statute brought legal denotation to terms such as "peace office," "motor vehicle," "fleeing an officer," "death," and "bodily injury" among others. In February, 1999, the Minnesota House of Representatives introduced a bill requiring the Peace Officer Standards and Training (POST) Board to adopt "a statewide model policy governing the conduct of police pursuits of fleeing suspects and requires state and municipal law enforcement agencies to adopt local police pursuit policies in conformity with the state policy" (Minnesota House of Representatives File # H.F. 381, 1999, p. 1). This bill also created two new programs for distributing tire deflation devices and driving simulators, along with monetary appropriations to be used for these programs.

Later in that same year, the Minnesota House of Representatives placed into law Minnesota Statute § 626.8458 (1999) requiring that, "By July 1, 1999, the board shall adopt a new or revised model policy governing the conduct of peace officers who are in pursuit of a vehicle being operated in violation of section 609.487" (p. 1). The bill stated that an agency's pursuit policy must include a statement describing the philosophy of the model policy: Namely that the safety of all persons involved in or by a police pursuit is of primary importance. In addition, the policy needed to "balance the risks of the pursuit to the public and peace officers with the consequences of failing to pursue" (p. 1).

The Minnesota statute detailed the necessity of including potentially hazardous pursuit tactics, the need to notify dispatch, responsibilities of the supervising officer, pursuing officer, and back-up officers. Jurisdictional considerations, report writing, and training were also specified in this statute.

In 1999, the state of California also took steps in placing into law a model policy for use in vehicular pursuits. California Penal Code § 13519.8 (2000) established guidelines for that state's model pursuit policy. The bill associated with this statute stated that, "The Commission shall implement, on or before November 1, 1994, a course or courses of instruction for the training of law enforcement officers in the handling of high-speed vehicle pursuits and shall also develop uniform, minimum guidelines for adoption by California law enforcement agencies for response to high-speed vehicle pursuits" (p. 1).

Similar to the Minnesota statute, the California Code stated that the guidelines to be established should include numerous factors inherent in a police vehicular pursuit, among which were initiation of the pursuit, driving tactics, speed limits, blocking, ramming, roadblocks, communications, air support, termination of pursuits, and environmental conditions. Also included in this model policy was the necessity for adequate training in the proper conduct of a vehicular pursuit. In addition, a safety caveat was included indicating, ". . . the need to balance the known offense and the need for immediate capture against the risks to officers and other citizens of a high-speed pursuit" (p. 1).

California has recently developed a bipartisan bill, SB 219, which would ultimately establish new standards for police vehicular pursuits. This new bill would require police agencies to adopt formal administrative procedures in the instance of any automobile collisions occurring as a result of any police pursuit (SB 219 Senate Bill-Bill Analysis, 2003). In addition, the state of Wisconsin has recently implemented Act 88, requiring more detailed reporting of all police pursuits, increased training for recruits, increasing the penalty for fleeing and eluding, and the creation of a law enforcement pursuit standards council (Witczak, 2003). According to Wisconsin Act 88, an increase in the pursuit training required of new police recruits will serve the multiple purposes of increasing the safety of all pursuits, making officers more aware of the consequences of pursuits, and increasing the public's awareness of the penalties associated with fleeing and eluding a law enforcement officer (Witczak, 2003).

Currently, the statewide policies that are in effect are still too young to have been tested in the long-term benefit of establishing a uniform policy within a state. If the benefits of statewide pursuit policies are to be reaped, an extensive analysis of the occurrence of accidents, injuries, fatalities, and property damage must be completed. Only upon a determination of whether the risks posed by police vehicular pursuits can be ascertained will the true effectiveness of statewide pursuit policies be understood. If statewide policies decrease exposure to liability and negligence for a department in conjunction with improved safety considerations for the officer, suspect, and general public, there is little doubt that more policymakers, legislators, and department commanders will begin to work in conjunction to implement additional uniform, statewide policies.

While the debate regarding the development of a nation wide pursuit policy continues to be bantered about, there are other possibilities that have been proposed to make vehicular pursuits completely unnecessary. In September, 1997, a proposal was introduced to the U.S. Senate regarding the development of a wireless Vehicle Intercept communication technology aimed at curbing the need for officers to pursue fleeing suspects (Eisenberg & Fitzpatrick, 1996; Congressional Record, 104th Congress, 1997). This device is designed to identify the fleeing suspect's automobile using a combination of the vehicle identification number and speed, ultimately disabling the car, preventing the need for the officer to pursue. The Vehicle Intercept device will operate at 260-470 MHz and will automatically retrieve the vehicle identification number and speed of the suspect's automobile. The pursuing officer will then provide the dispatch officer with the necessary data. The dispatch officer will then query a database to locate the suspect's car, sending an encrypted key to the criminal's automobile, thus resetting the engine's RPMs to 800, bringing the vehicle to an idle state.

This system, while still in the design and prototype stage, is intended to prevent abuse by the general public through a requirement of a multi-user interface and 128-bit security encryption. The device will stop the suspect's vehicle while allowing all nearby vehicles freedom from any ill affect. This new technology will prevent suspects from engaging in high-speed flight from police. While there are critics who may voice concern over the effects of a "Big Brother" government, the increased safety factor associated with such a technological advancement in law enforcement might quell any uneasiness regarding such a project.

CONCLUSION

As the trend of statewide pursuit policies continues to be accepted, the importance of safety is never so evident. Each state bill or law states the necessity for a pursuing officer to balance the importance of apprehending the suspect against the risks to the public, themselves, and the suspect. As the statewide policies are designed to limit a department's exposure to claims of liability and negligence, an emphasis on safety is logical. If the risks to the public or the officer outweigh the necessity to apprehend the suspect, then continuing with the pursuit is not justified and further pursuit action should be terminated.

Currently, the statewide policies that are in effect are still too young to have been tested in the long-term benefit of establishing a uniform policy within a state. If the benefits of statewide pursuit policies are to be reaped, an extensive analysis of the occurrence of accidents, injuries, fatalities, and property damage must be completed. Only upon a determination of whether the risks posed by police vehicular pursuits can be ascertained will the true effectiveness of statewide pursuit policies be understood. If statewide policies decrease exposure to liability and negligence for a department in conjunction with improved safety considerations for the officer, suspect, and general public, there is little doubt that more policymakers, legislators, and department commanders will begin to implement their own uniform, statewide policies.

REFERENCES

Allen, J. (1973). *American society: Inquiry into civic issues.* New York: American Book.

Alpert, G., & Dunham, R. (1988). Research on police pursuits: Applications for law enforcement. *American Journal of Police, 7:* 123–131.

Britz, M., & Payne, D. (1994). Policy implications for law enforcement pursuit driving. *American Journal of Police, 13*(1): 113–142.

Carter, D. L. (1986). *Police deviance.* Cincinnati, OH: Anderson.

Charles, M., Falcone, D., & Wells, E. (1992a). *Police pursuit in pursuit of policy: The pursuit issue, legal and literature review, and an empirical study.* Washington, D.C.: AAA Foundation for Traffic Safety.

Congressional record proceedings and debates (1997). 104th Congress, 1st session.

Connecticut House of Representatives (1997). Substitute House Bill No. 5186: Public Act No. 97–310.

Eisenberg, C., & Fitzpatrick, C. (1996). Police practice: An alternative to police pursuits. *FBI Law Enforcement Bulletin, 65*(8): 16–20.

Hicks, W. L. (2001). *Police vehicular pursuits: An analysis of state police and state highway patrol policies.* Unpublished doctoral, dissertation, Michigan State University, East Lansing, MI.

Johnson, P., Aldrich, J., Miller, G., Ostrom, C., & Rhode, D. (1990). *American government: People, institutions, and policies.* Boston: Houghton Mifflin.

Minnesota House of Representatives (1999). House research bill summary H.F. 381.

New Jersey Task Force on Police Vehicular Pursuit Policy (1999). *Vehicular pursuit: New Jersey Police vehicular pursuit policy.*

Payne, D. (1993). *Preliminary findings from the Michigan Emergency response study: Phase II. A report to the Michigan State Police training division.* East Lansing, MI: Michigan

State University.

Physician for Automotive Safety (1968). *Rapid pursuit by the police: Causes, hazards, consequences: A national pattern is evident.* New York: Physicians for Automotive Safety.

State of California (2000). Cal. Pen. Code § 13519.8.

State of California, State Senate Bill 219 (2002).

State of California, State Senate Bill 219 Bill Analysis (2003).

State of Minnesota (1999). Minn. Stat. § 609.487.

State of Minnesota (1999). Minn. Stat. § 626.8458.

Witczak, T. (2003). Proactive pursuits policies. *Law & Order, 51*(7): 131.

INDEX

Charles C Thomas

PUBLISHER • LTD.

P.O. Box 19265
Springfield, IL 62794-9265

COMING SOON!